COMPACT GU

LIS

for less

GW00832050

includes
**DISCOUNT
COUPONS FOR
ATTRACTIONS
& MUSEUMS**

the guidebook that pays for itself in one day

Lisbon
for less

Compact
Guide

Publisher Information

First published in Great Britain in 1999 by Metropolis International (UK) Ltd.

ISBN 1 901811 55 7

COPYRIGHT

DISCLAIMER

Assessments of attractions, hotels, museums and so forth are based on the author's impressions and therefore contain an element of subjective opinion that may not reflect the opinion of the publishers.

The contents of this publication are believed to be correct at the time of printing. However, details such as opening times will change over time. We would advise you to call ahead to confirm important information.

All organizations offering discounts in this guidebook have a contract with the publisher to give genuine discounts to holders of valid *for less* vouchers.

The publisher and/or its agents will not be responsible if any establishment breaches its contract (although it will attempt to secure compliance) or if any establishment changes ownership and the new owners refuse to honour the contract.

Care has been taken to ensure that discounts are only offered at reputable establishments, however, the publisher and/or its agents cannot accept responsibility for the quality of merchandise or service provided, nor for errors or inaccuracies in this guidebook.

The publisher will not be held responsible for any loss, damage, injury, expense or inconvenience sustained by any person, howsoever caused, as a result of information or advice contained in this guide except insofar as the law prevents the exclusion of such liability.

PUBLISHER

Metropolis International
222 Kensal Road
London W10 5BN
England

Telephone:
+44-(0)181-964-4242
(After May 2000, tel:
+44-(0)20-8964-4242)

Fax:
+44-(0)181-964-4141
(After May 2000, fax:
+44-(0)20-8964-4141)

E-mail:
admin@for-less.com

Web site:
http://www.for-less.com

ABBREVIATIONS

☎   Telephone Number
🕐   Opening times

Contents

HOW TO OBTAIN DISCOUNTS

Many of the museums and attractions in this guide offer discounts to holders of this book.

Museums and attractions which offer a discount are highlighted in pink in the text and designated by the following symbol in the margins:

To obtain your discount, simply hand in the appropriate voucher from the back of the book when you purchase your ticket.

Introduction to Lisbon

No introduction to Lisbon can begin without reference to the great earthquake of 1755, which destroyed many of the city's buildings. The **Marquês de Pombal**'s handling of this catastrophic disaster says much about the national character of the Portuguese.

A friendly, multi-cultural, southern European people with a passion for good food, pets and children and a penchant for common sense and *sang froid*, Lisbon itself reflects all these features. It has been called the last city of the old world and the first of the new.

Lisbon's expansion westward is limited by the neighbouring coastal resorts of **Estoril** and **Cascais** and the Atlantic Ocean beyond. The **River Tejo** forms a natural barrier on the south side of the city. However, there are now two bridges across the Tejo, and new urban development is springing up opposite the old city.

The main city is divided into many neighbourhoods, but most sites of interest are concentrated into just a few areas. In this guide, the city is divided into four areas: **Baixa and Alfama**, **Bairro Alto and Estrela**, **North Lisbon** and **Belém**.

Alfama is the oldest surviving part of Lisbon. This is the portion of the city that was administered by the Moors until they

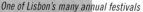
One of Lisbon's many annual festivals

Torre de Belém

were defeated in the siege of **Castelo de São Jorge** (page 18) in 1147. The castle, which is built in the Moorish architectural style, retains its central importance to Lisbon's geography, and can be seen from almost anywhere in the city.

The cathedral of **Sé** (page 21) was built by King Afonso Henriques in 1150 as a defensive measure to dissuade the Moors from planning a counter-attack on Lisbon. It is the final resting place of **St. Vincent**, Lisbon's patron saint.

Other famous churches in the Alfama area are **Santa Engrácia** (page 24), which took 284 years to finish, and **São Vicente de Fora** (page 22), which holds the Bragança dynasty's royal crypt.

Alfama retains its Moorish heritage in its old city walls, its narrow atmospheric alleyways and its often humble dwellings. Life here is very traditional, with a sense of the exuberant spirit of the Kasbah in its incessant music, markets and shops.

With the total destruction of the **Baixa** area (the 'low' quarter) in the 1755 earthquake, the Marquês de Pombal was given the task of rebuilding it. His grid of elegant streets ran from the meeting-point square, **Rossio**, in the north (page 14) to the palace and river port of **Praça do Comércio** in the south (page 10).

Did You Know ...?

The Portuguese learnt the technique of making *ajulejos*, the lovely painted tiles to be seen all over the city, from the Moors in the 15th century.

Padrão dos Descobrimentos

These streets are lined with either the original neo-classical buildings or newer blocks of a complementary style. It is the commercial centre of Lisbon, and by day it is packed with people working, walking or enjoying a coffee in one of the many cafés.

Perhaps the most chic part of the Baixa area is **Chiado**, known as a haunt of writers and intellectuals. Largely razed to the ground by fire in 1988, this retail district of high fashion and elegance has been lovingly rebuilt.

Don't Miss ...

The **Castelo de Sao Jorge** (page 18), a beautifully restored citadel with stunning views and lovely gardens.

Several spectacular funicular railways and lifts, such as the **Elevador de Santa Justa** (page 14), connect Baixa to the 'high quarter', **Bairro Alto**, which overhangs it. Containing several of Lisbon's hills, it gained in affluence and importance when many of the city's wealthy residents settled in the neighbourhood after the 1755 disaster. The Bairro Alto and its neighbour **Estrela** remain affluent residential areas to this day.

Priceless Portuguese paintings and sculptures are contained at Bairro Alto's **Museu Nacional de Arte Antiga** (page 29), and the **Igreja de São Roque** (page 16) is an opulent jewel of a church. Estrela is more residential, but the district's domed **Basílica** (page 27) and the gardens which surround it (page 28) are well worth a visit.

The **North Lisbon** area is a reasonably new district, so its attractions tend to be modern in nature. The area is dominated by the **Fundação Calouste Gulbenkian** complex, a group of excellent museums and arts centres (page 32).

North Lisbon boasts many other museums, but its dominant features include the massive **Parque Eduardo VII** (page 31) and the **Aqueduto das Águas Livres** (page 34).

Belém is set apart from the rest of central Lisbon. Situated at the mouth of the River Tejo, this green suburb of the city was the departure point for the great seafaring expeditions of the Age of Discovery. The success of these voyages led the royal family to commission monuments which have since become part of the national psyche.

The **Mosteiro dos Jerónimos** (page 43) and the **Torre de Belém** (page 39) are two such sites, both celebrations of the maritime Manueline architectural style. Belém was once home to the royal family, but is now a haven for museum-goers, coffee-drinkers and walkers.

Currently, Lisbon is experiencing its busiest period of change since Pombal's time, and is benefiting from political stability and economic prosperity.

In 1998 the city hosted **Expo 98**, an international exhibition celebrating its important maritime history, which brought an influx of new interest and tourism.

IF YOU DO ONE THING . . .

1. If you visit one museum . . .
Museu Calouste Gulbenkian (page 32)

2. If you visit one church . . .
Sé cathedral (page 21)

3. If you take one *elevador* ride . . .
Elevador de Santa Justa (page 14)

4. If you go on one excursion . . .
Sintra (page 46)

5. If you take one walk . . .
Parque Eduardo VII (page 31)

6. If you dine in one restaurant . . .
Casa do Leão (page 50)

7. If you go to one art gallery . . .
Museu de Arte Popular (page 40)

8. If you go to one bar . . .
Café Martinho da Arcada (page 51)

9. If you go to one attraction . . .
Mosteiro dos Jeronimos (page 43)

10. If you go shopping in one area . .
Chaido (page 52)

History of Lisbon

According to myth, **Odysseus** founded Lisbon on his way home from Troy. It is more likely that a sea-faring people called the **Phoenicians** founded Lisbon as a trading post for copper and tin in about 1200BC. The **Romans** eventually took control of the region in 205BC, ousting the **Lusitanian** tribes which had settled there, and making Lisbon the administrative capital of the area.

On the collapse of the Roman empire Portugal was occupied by **barbarian tribes** from northern Europe. The city fell into decay until the **Moors** invaded from north Africa in AD711 and developed Lisbon as a trading port.

Reflections

'We must bury the dead and feed the living' - the Marquês de Aloma after the 1755 earthquake

The Moors fortified Lisbon against attack, but the walled defences and stronghold of the **Castelo de São Jorge** (page 18) were no match for the forces of **Afonso Henriques**, who became Portugal's first Catholic king in 1147. The new king reinforced the city against Moorish retaliation by building the **Sé** cathedral (page 21). By 1256, Lisbon had grown so much in importance that it took over from Coimbra as the capital city.

The reputation of Lisbon as a centre of culture dates back to the reign of **King Dinis**. He established the city's university in 1290, increased trade with the rest of Europe and extended the city limits into Baixa. By 1415, Portugal had enough confidence and wealth to conquer Ceuta (part of modern-day Morocco) on the north African coast. Advanced ship-building methods and a need to seek new sources of food persuaded **Prince Henry the Navigator** and other patrons to fund the expeditions of the Age of Discovery.

Perhaps the most famous journey was made in 1498, when **Vasco da Gama** reached India by sailing around Africa. During the 16th century more routes were discovered, providing access to the Far East, South America and Canada, and the Portuguese soon controlled the trade routes in the Indian Ocean.

As Portugal's wealth increased, so the

church became more powerful, and by the 16th century non-Catholic believers were embroiled in the **Inquisition**'s reign of terror. The power of the Inquisition was further strengthened by a period of direct rule by Spain from 1580 to 1640.

The great earthquake disaster of 1755 destroyed most of Lisbon while its people were at mass one Sunday morning. Suddenly the city's priorities changed. José I gave the **Marquês de Pombal** the responsibility of rebuilding the city. Pombal's grid-pattern set the style for many modern city layouts, such as those found in America.

Napoleon's invasion of Portugal at the start of the 19th century caused the royal family to flee to Brazil. Britain saw off Napoleon's threat but exacted a heavy price by forcing the Portuguese to allow trade with Portugal's colonies. The royals returned, but in 1908, the autocratic **King Carlos** and his eldest son were assassinated. The establishment of a republic followed in 1910.

After years of unstable government, **Salazar** seized office in 1926, keeping his fascist regime neutral during World War II. While Lisbon had money spent on it, the rest of Portugal suffered. A peaceful revolution took place in 1974 to establish a modern democracy, and investment poured into Portugal after the country joined the European Union in 1986. Recent years have seen Lisbon develop into a fully-fledged European capital, a process highlighted by its hosting of the **Expo** in 1998.

A ferry in the harbour

Baixa and Alfama

Baixa's **Praça do Comércio** is the former site of the royal palace. Manuel I relocated the monarch's residence from **Castelo de São Jorge** (page 18) to this site in 1511, to take advantage of low-lying ground on

Praça do Comércio

the north bank of the River Tejo. He converted the area into a harbour which he used for welcoming foreign dignitaries.

The original palace was destroyed in the great earthquake of 1755, but the Marquês de Pombal rebuilt this square as the centrepiece of his plans for the city's restoration. Three sides of the square were taken up with new palace buildings, which are now used for government administration.

Praça do Comércio

The square is a focal point of Lisbon's history. In 1908, King Carlos and his eldest son, Luís Filipe, were assassinated here, and in 1974 the square was the scene of the bloodless Carnation Revolution which overthrew Marcelo Caetano's government.

The central statue depicts José I, who was king at the time of the earthquake, on horseback. The riverbank site is still used as the landing point for the ferry from **Cacilhas** on the south bank of the river (page 49).

The **Rua Augusta** leads off from the Praça do Comércio through the triumphal **Arco da Rua Augusta**, built in 1873 to commemorate the city's recovery from the earthquake.

The **Praça do Município** lies to the north-west of the much larger Praça do Comércio. The former square houses the neo-classical-style **City Hall** on its eastern side. Built in 1874, it contains the Marquês de Pombal's original architectural plans for rebuilding Lisbon. These plans were themselves rescued from damage in 1988 during a fire in the Chiado quarter of the city. The Portuguese Republic was formally declared here on October 5th 1910.

In the centre of the square stands an 18th-century, twisted pillar with a banded sphere at the top, typical of the Manueline style.

Excavation work carried out during the building of the **Banco Comercial Português** revealed layers of Lisbon's ancient history, collectively known as the **Núcleo Arqueológico**.

Banco Comercial Português

Rua Augusta 62-74

The **Rua dos Correeiros** entrance leads to a display of remains from a Roman fish-preserving plant, a 5th-century Christian burial ground and of pottery from Moorish settlements.

The **Rua Augusta** entrance reveals a network of underground tunnels, galleries and baths which comprised a 1st-century AD Roman spa. The site is dedicated to Aesclaepius, the Roman god of

Arco da Rua Augusta

Museu do Chiado

Rua Serpa Pinto 4-6
☎ 01-343 21 48
🕐 Tue: 2pm-6pm. Wed-
Sun: 10-6pm. Mon:
closed.
Admission charge.

Mercado da Ribeira

Avenida 24 de Julho
🕐 Mon-Sat: 6am-2pm.
Sun: closed.

medicine. Local myth suggests the clear
waters here have general healing powers.

The National Museum of Contemporary Art
changed its name along with its location
in 1994 to the **Museu do Chiado**. This was
because its range of art, dating from 1850
to 1950, could no longer be called
contemporary. Its new home is a restored
19th-century biscuit factory, and the
museum's 12 rooms explore different
themes ranging from the Romantic to the
Modern movements.

The art in the museum is mainly
Portuguese, but there are some pieces by
Rodin and a few other examples from
French artists. Local painters include
António Teixeira Lopez, António Costa
Pinheiro (both strong on landscapes) and
Carlos Botelho and José Malhoa (who
painted Lisbon scenes).

The **Teatro Nacional de São Carlos**
replaced an earlier opera house which was
irreparably damaged in the 1755
earthquake. Built in 1792–5 by José de
Costa e Silva, the new theatre design was
inspired by La Scala in Milan and San
Carlo in Naples. The theatre is noted for
its beautiful rococo interior and its lovely
facade.

Operas are staged at the theatre from
September to June, but the venue also
hosts ballets and orchestral concerts at

Praça do Comércio

Largo do Carmo

other times of the year. Many performances here sell out quickly. *(Rua Serpa Pinto 9, ☎ 01 346 5914. ⏰ Admission to performances only.)*

The main market in Lisbon is the **Mercado de Ribeira**, sandwiched between the Cais do Sodré railway station to the south and the funicular Elevador da Bica to the north. Its busiest time of day is early morning when the produce is at its freshest. The market, covered by a domed roof, teems with people selling food of all descriptions. The fish hall and meat slabs are not for the squeamish as the food is prepared and presented *in situ*. The upper gallery is noted for its range of flowers, vegetables and spices.

The arch at the northern tip of the Mercado de Ribeira houses the funicular, **Elevador da Bica**. The railway is a steep yet exhilarating climb from its base at Rua de São Paulo to Rua do Loreto in Biarro Alto at the top.

The **Convento do Carmo** was built in 1423 by Dom Nuno Álvares Pereira, the military commander who served João I before spending the rest of his life here. His monastery was partially ruined in the great earthquake of 1755, when the roof caved in during a celebration of mass, killing many worshippers. Before this disaster,

Elevador da Bica

Rua de São Paulo and
Rua do Loreto
⏰ Mon-Sat: 7am-11pm.
Sun: 9am-11pm.
Admission charge.

Convento do Carmo

Largo do Carmo
☎ 01 346 04 73
⏰ Tue-Sun: 10am-6pm
(Apr-Sep). Tue-Sun:
10am-1pm, 2pm-5pm
(Oct-Mar).
Admission charge.

View of Lisbon from the Elevador de Santa Justa

Elevador de Santa Justa

Rua de Santa Justa and
Largo do Carmo
☎ 01 346 04 73
🕐 Mon-Sat: 7am-11pm.
Sun: 9am-11pm.
Admission charge.

the building was the largest church in
Lisbon.

The remaining structure consists of Gothic
arches, walls and buttresses. The nave is
open to the elements, with roses growing
up the aisle and around the columns. The
former altar stands next to two important
carved tombs: Fernando I and Gonçalo de
Sousa, chancellor to Henry the Navigator.
The ruins provide a refuge for stray cats
and a beautiful backdrop for occasional
open-air concerts.

The chancel of the original church
retained its roof in the earthquake. This
portion is now the **Museu Arqueológico do
Carmo**, housing an eclectic mixture of
artefacts. There is no consistent theme to
the collection of sarcophagi, flints, coins,
ceramics and arrowheads displayed in
glass cases.

Notable exhibits include a Brazilian
sculpture in jasper of the Virgin Mary,
some South American tribal mummies
(and trophy heads of local natives) and
fragments of Roman and Visigoth tombs.

Built in 1902 by Raoul Mesnier du
Ponsard, an apprentice of Eiffel, the
Elevador de Santa Justa is an iron
passenger lift linking Baixa to Bairra Alto.
The walkway and café offer spectacular
views of the city.

Rossio has been at the heart of Lisbon life
for over 600 years. Formerly a village on

the city's edge until the 20th century, the square attracted artists and writers to its cafés. The monument dedicated to Pedro IV in the centre of the square is probably a statue of Maximillian of Mexico which was renamed in 1867 after the latter was assassinated.

To the east of Rossio, **Praça da Figueira** was the site of Lisbon's main market from before the 1755 earthquake until the 1950s. It is now a square of shops and cafés, with an equestrian statue of João I by Leopoldo de Almeida (1971) at its centre. Before the earthquake it was also the site of Lisbon's main hospital.

The **Teatro Nacional Dona Maria II** is the grandest building in Rossio, named after Pedro IV's daughter. It was built is 1840 by the Italian architect, Fortunado Lodi, and was restored to its former splendour after a fire in 1964. The theatre stands on the site of the Inquisitor-General's headquarters, which would have overlooked the many public executions which took place in the square.

To the east of Rossio and north of Praça da Figueira lies **Igreja de São Domingos**, a church in a quiet square comprised of food stores, clothing shops and jewellers.

The church has played a major role in Lisbon's history. From 1540 to 1767, it was where the judgements of the

Teatro Nacional Dona Maria II

Rossio
☎ 01-342 22 10
🕐 Performances only.

Igreja de São Domingos

Largo de São Domingos
🕐 Mon-Sun: 8am-7pm.

Rossio

Igreja de São Roque

Largo Trindade Coelho
☎ 01-348 03 61
Church:
⊕ Mon-Sun: 8.30am-
5pm.
Museum:
⊕ Mon-Sun: 10am-5pm.

Largo de São Domingos

Capela de São João Baptista

Largo Trindade Coelho
☎ 01-348 03 61
⊕ Mon-Sun: 8.30am-
5pm.

Inquisition were read out to the public. The Inquisition was a tribunal of the Roman Catholic church which demanded rigid adherence to the orthodoxies of the Counter Reformation.

Answerable only to the Pope, the Inquisitor-General claimed the right to extract public confessions of heretical belief or non-belief in the Roman Catholic faith. His 'Act of the Faith' judgements (*auto-da-fé*) were followed by torture and/ or execution in Rossio or the Largo de São Domingos.

The original 13th-century church was devastated by the 1755 earthquake and Johann Friedrich Ludovice, an 18th-century German-Portuguese architect, was commissioned to rebuild it.

A catastrophic fire in 1959 destroyed the former glory of the church's interior but a recent restoration has now been completed. The visitor cannot fail to be impressed by the cavernous appearance of the nave and the charred pillars, which have been left as a fitting reminder both of the 20th-century fire and the church's historic past.

The square, **Largo de São Domingos**, remains a popular local meeting place, especially for the city's resident African population. It also contains several *ginginha* (cherry brandy) bars where the local firewater can be sampled.

The plain facade of the **Igreja de São Roque** belies the splendour of its interior. The church was founded in the 16th century by Jesuits on the foundations of a hermitage.

The church is famous for its chapels, notably that dedicated to John the Baptist (see below). The **Capela de São Roque** is the oldest and hosts excellent examples of Florentine *azulejo* (tiling). The **Chapel of the Holy Family** boasts an exquisite wood carving. The ceiling gives the optical illusion of a dome, depicting scenes from the Apocalypse and incidents in the life of the Jesuit missionary, St. Francis Xavier.

The **Museu de Arte Sacra** is entered through the Igreja de São Roque and is

Elevador da Glória

housed in what used to be the church's convent. The museum is a treasure trove of religious artefacts from this building and other Jesuit churches and monasteries from around Europe. Its displays chart the history of the Igreja de São Roque and of the Jesuit movement in general.

Examples of baroque splendour in the museum include the priceless gold and lapis lazuli altar front of the Capela de São João, opulent mitres and richly embroidered vestments.

The **Capela de São João Baptista** is perhaps the world's most opulent chapel of its size. Commissioned by João V in 1742, the chapel was built in Rome before being dismantled and shipped to Lisbon. The chapel used the most expensive materials available.

The **Solar do Vinho do Porto** is a famous bar where more than 300 varieties of port can be sampled in the setting of a luxurious mansion house, once owned by the architect Ludovice. Port was 'invented' in the 17th century, when British merchants added brandy to the wine they were purchasing from the Douro region of Portugal to stop it going sour on the way home.

The recipe has been refined over the years, and much of port production is still under British control. The Solar do Vinho

Museu de Arte Sacra

Largo Trindade Coelho
☎ 01-348 03 61
🕐 Tue-Sun: 10am-1pm
and 2pm-5pm. Mon:
closed.
Admission charge.

Solar do Vinho do Porto

Rua de São Pedro de
Alcântara 45
☎ 01-347 57 07
🕐 Mon-Fri: 10am-
11.30pm. Sat: 11am-
10.30pm. Sun: closed.

do Porto keeps over 6,000 ports in its cellars.

The yellow carriages of the **Elevador da Glória** are a great way to travel up the São Pedro hill. Built in 1885, the highly decorative funicular was originally powered by water compression before converting to steam. Today it runs on electricity.

The **Miradouro de São Pedro de Alcântara** are gardens at the top of the hill which give a panoramic view of the Baixa region. The view is perhaps best at sunset after a ride on the funicular Elevador da Glória. The garden terrace is a popular meeting point.

The gardens commemorate the famous 19th-century editor, Eduardo Coelho, who founded the newspaper, *Diário de Notícias*, in premises on this site. Part of the memorial features a boy selling copies of the newspaper. The industry has now moved to more modern premises in the west.

The **Castelo de São Jorge** is visible from every part of Lisbon and is central to the city's history. The original Roman fort on the site was strengthened during Moorish rule in the 9th century.

The Christian attack on the Muslim-led castle in 1147 resulted in the overthrow of the Moors and the installation of Afonso Henriques as the first Portuguese king.

Elevador da Glória

Praça dos Restauradores and Rua de São Pedro de Alcântara
🕐 Mon-Sat: 7am-11pm
Sun: closed.
Admission charge.

View across Lisbon from the Castelo de São Jorge

There is a statue of him at the front gate.

Afonso Henriques set about converting the citadel into a royal residence, and the Moors were banished to the Mouraria quarter outside the castle walls. The ruins of the **Alcáçova** you can see in the Castelo today are a much-renovated version of the original Moorish palace.

In 1511, Manuel I built a more luxurious palace near the River Tejo at what is now the Praça do Comércio (page 10), and apart from one interlude during Sebastião's reign between 1557 and 1578, the Portuguese monarchs never lived in the Castelo again. Instead, it was used variously as a theatre, a prison and an arsenal.

The 1755 earthquake destroyed the ramparts. These were restored as late as 1938 by Salazar, an act symbolising the strength of the Portuguese nation.

The view from the battlements should not be missed, and the grounds inside the castle walls contain the tiny **Santa Cruz** quarter of cobbled streets and compact houses, together with a 12th-century church and several restaurants.

The **Museu da Marioneta** houses a compact yet fascinating collection of puppets, ranging from tiny finger puppets to full-scale puppet costumes.

The museum contains an excellent selection of characters from 17th- and 18th-century theatre and opera productions. It also houses traditional 19th-century Portuguese puppets and an interesting selection of Asian exhibits.

Some of these beautifully crafted artefacts have grotesque features which may frighten the very young, but older children are well catered for by the museum. Videos of puppet shows are screened at regular intervals and live performances are often staged in the tiny theatre at weekends.

The **Largo das Portas do Sol** is the square which contains one of the seven original gates to the Moorish city walls: the so-called 'sun gateway'. The view of the River

Miradouro de São Pedro de Alcântara

Rua de São Pedro de Alcântara

Castelo de São Jorge

Porta de São Jorge, Rua do Chão de Feira
🕑 Mon-Sun: 9am-11pm.

Museu da Marioneta

Largo Rodrigues de Freitas 19a
☎ 01-886 57 94
🕑 Tue-Sun: 10am-1pm and 3pm-6pm. Mon: closed.
Admission charge.

Sé

Tejo and the Alfama district from here is breathtaking. A statue of St Vincent, clutching a boat and two ravens, the symbol of Lisbon, stands in the square's centre.

The banker Ricardo do Espírito Santo Silva set up a Foundation, a research institute, and the **Museu-Escola de Artes Decorativas** in 1953. The museum is housed in the Palácio Azurara, which he had originally purchased to house his own private art collection.

The collection consists of Portuguese furniture, textiles and household goods from the 17th and 18th centuries. The building has beautiful original ceilings and *azulejo* (tile) decorations, and also contains artisans' workshops where traditional craft-making techniques are demonstrated.

The museum's intention is to improve public awareness of Portuguese craft and to make sure these skills are not forgotten.

The **Igreja de Santa Luzia** stands on the side of a steep hillside. This small church is noted for its balustraded *miradouro* (belvedere), which gives welcome rest and shade to walkers. Local men often play cards in the garden and the views of the river and harbour below are spectacular.

The church itself is known for the 18th-century blue and white *azulejo* (tile) panels on its Moorish south wall. One picture shows the Praça do Comércio (page 10) as it would have been before

Museu-Escola de Artes Decorativas

Largo das Portas do Sol 2
☎ 01-886 21 83
🕐 Wed-Tue: 10am-5pm.
Mon: closed.
Admission charge.
2 admissions for the price of 1 with voucher on page 69.

the 1755 earthquake. The other depicts the story of Martim Moniz, a brave knight who was killed during the siege of the Castelo de São Jorge in 1147 (page 18).

The **Igreja de São Miguel** is one of the oldest surviving churches in Lisbon, established in the 17th century. Badly damaged in the 1755 earthquake, it was subsequently restored. The most notable example of its simple yet exquisite décor is the ceiling, which is made of Brazilian jacaranda wood. *(Rua de São Miguel.)*

Moors from North Africa ruled Lisbon from the 5th century AD until the Christian assault on the Castelo de São Jorge in 1147. One of the best preserved sections of city wall surrounding the Alfama district from this period is the ruined **Moorish Tower** which takes up one side of the Largo de São Rafael.

Once Afonso Henriques had defeated the Moors in 1147, he was keen to cement the new Christian regime by constructing a cathedral in the city. In 1150 he commissioned the building of **Sé** (short for *Sedes Episcopalis*, or bishop's seat) and made the English crusader, Gilbert of Hastings, the first bishop of Lisbon.

As the king was worried about enemy reprisals, the original cathedral was built like a fortress. Sé retains these features today, even though it has been renovated many times over the centuries. The building was devastated three times in the 14th century by earth tremors and collapsed once more in the great earthquake of 1755, losing the 18th-century embellishments given to the church by João V.

Today the interior contains nine Gothic chapels, a cloister, a treasury and the cathedral's original font, which was used to baptise St. Anthony in 1195. The best-known of the chapels is the **Capela de Santo Ildefonso**, which houses the 14th century sarcophagi of Lopo Fernandes Pacheco, his wife and their dogs.

An adjacent chancel contains the sarcophagi of Afonso IV and his wife, Dona Beatriz. The first chapel contains a nativity scene by Machado de Castro made

Igreja de Santa Luzia

Rua do Limoeiro

Igreja de São Miguel

Rua de São Miguel

Moorish Tower

Largo de São Rafael

Sé

Largo da Sé
☎ 01-886 67 52
🕐 Mon–Sun: 9am–5pm.
Admission charge.

Santo António à Sé and the Museu Antoniano

Largo de S. António à Sé
Church:
☎ 01-886 91 45
🕐 Mon–Sun: 8am–
7.30pm.
Museum:
☎ 01-886 04 47
🕐 Tue–Sun: 10am–1pm
and 2pm–6pm. Mon:
closed.
Admission charge.

Casa dos Bicos

Rua dos Bacalhoeiros
☎ 01-888 48 27
🕐 Open for temporary
exhibitions only.

The cloisters are noted for the Roman remains found during an archaeological dig. The treasury consists of a collection of robes, silverware and illustrated manuscripts. Its most important item is a casket containing the remains of St. Vincent, patron saint of Lisbon, which were brought back to the city by boat in 1173. Legend has it that the journey was watched over by two ravens, thus giving rise to this emblem of the city.

The little church of **Santo António à Sé** was given an overhaul in 1995 for the 800th anniversary of the birth of St. Anthony, who is revered for bringing good luck to personal relationships. Newly-wed couples often pose for photographs outside the church and offer flowers to the saint. The crypt is the only part of the original church left standing by the 1755 earthquake.

The adjoining **Museu Antoniano** commemorates the life, work and heritage of St. Anthony, through its artworks and artefacts.

The **Casa dos Bicos** was built in 1523 for Brás de Albuquerque, the then President of the Senate. Its name derives from the diamond-shaped studs which protrude from the front wall of the house, a style popular in 16th-century Mediterranean architecture.

The top two storeys of the house were destroyed in the 1755 earthquake. Their renovation was completed in 1980, using contemporary illustrations, engravings and *azulejo* (tile) panels.

For a time it was used as a warehouse for salting fish, but the upper floors are now the offices of the Discoveries Commission, an organisation set up to oversee exhibitions and events commemorating Vasco da Gama's discovery of the sea route to India in 1498.

The lower floors function as a gallery for hosting temporary exhibitions of architectural artefacts.

Construction of the **Mosteiro de São Vicente de Fora** began after the 12th century crusaders under Alfonso

Igreja da Santa Engrácia

Henriques vowed to build a monastery for St. Vincent, the patron Saint of Lisbon, if they won a decisive battle against the Moors. They were successful, Lisbon was reclaimed, and building commenced.

The church lies on the site where Afonso Henriques had pitched camp during the successful siege of Lisbon. It was rebuilt in 1627 by the architect Filippo Terzi, a devotee of the Italianate style. The facade is simple, save for three statues – of Saints Vincent, Augustine and Sebastian – and some towers.

The church's interior in noted for the baroque wooden statues, organ and altar canopy by Machado de Castro, all of which survived the collapse of the dome during the earthquake of 1755.

An Augustine monastery is attached to the church. This features some ruined cloisters, famed for their 18th-century *azulejo* panels depicting countryside scenes from the La Fontaine fables and stories of the siege of the Castelo de São Jorge (page 18) by Afonso Henriques and the Crusaders.

A passage at the back of the church leads to an old out-building, converted in 1885 into a pantheon to the Bragança dynasty. This contains sarcophagi of all but two Portuguese monarchs from João IV to

**Mosteiro de
São Vicente de Fora**

Largo de São Vicente
☎ 01-886 25 44
Church:
🕐 Mon-Sun: 9am-12.30pm and 3pm-6.30pm.
Pantheon of the Bragança Dynasty:
🕐 Tue-Sun: 10am-5.30pm. Mon: closed.

of cork, terracotta and wood and dating from 1766.

Manuel II, who died exiled in England in 1932. Perhaps the most poignant tomb is that of Carlos I and his eldest son, Luís Filipe, assassinated in the Praça do Comércio in 1908 (page 10). A ghostly stone mourner stands silently praying over the tomb.

Igreja de Santa Engrácia

Campo de Santa Clara
☎ 01-888 15 29
🕐 Tue-Sun: 10am-5pm.
Mon: closed.
Admission charge.

The dome of the **Igreja de Santa Engrácia** is a striking landmark on the Lisbon skyline. The original church fell down during a storm in 1681 and reconstruction of the church began the following year, but it was not until 1966 (some 284 years later) that the building work was finally completed. This famous delay entered the Portuguese language as the proverb: '*Obras de Santa Engrácia*' meaning 'A Santa Engrácia project never gets done'.

The interior of the church gives the impression of vast space. At the top of the dome you can enjoy a superb view of the city.

Santa Engrácia is now home to the **Panteão Nacional**, the national pantheon for non-royalty. There are six marble cenotaphs to the greatest heroes in Portuguese history and other tombs of famous politicians and cultural icons.

The main cenotaphs include commemorations of Vasco de Gama (the famous explorer, tradesman and discoverer of India), Henry the Navigator (the third son of João I who was the financial patron of many 15th-century expeditions), and Luís de Camões (the national poet whose most famous work, *Os Lusíadas*, told the story of the Discoveries).

The most recent addition to the pantheon is General Humberto Delgado, a freedom fighter murdered in 1965 by Salazar's secret police.

Feira da Ladra

Campo de Santa Clara
🕐 Tue and Sat: 7.30am-1pm.

The **Feira da Ladra** (translated as 'Thieves Market') is held twice every week in the Campo da Santa Clara. For over 100 years traders have sold tourist goods in the Alfama district, ranging from African colonial mementoes to second-hand junk. Bargains are hard to come by these days as an increasing number of tourists flock to the market.

The building which houses the **Museu Militar** was a 16th-century cannon foundry before being used as a warehouse for the Portuguese army. In 1842 it became a museum and now contains the largest collection of artillery artefacts in the world. The museum covers the period from the siege of the Castelo de São Jorge in 1147 (page 18) up to World War I.

Exhibits show the evolution of weaponry in Portuguese history from flints to rifles. Star attractions include the contraption used to erect the statue of João I in the Praça do Comércio (page 10) and the carriage used to build the triumphal arch (at the north side of the square).

The **Museu Nacional do Azulejo** is located in a former convent, the Convento da Madre de Deus. The convent was established in 1509, but the last of the nuns died in the mid 19th century. The cloisters now host a museum dedicated to the art of *azulejo*. This traditional craft of painting tiles evolved from Moorish and Spanish influences into a distinctly Portuguese art form.

The museum charts the evolution of the craft from the 14th century onwards. Pride of place goes to the 36 metre (140 foot) long, horizontal panel showing a panoramic view of Lisbon before the earthquake struck the city in 1755.

Museu Militar

Largo do Museu da Artilharia
☎ 01-888 21 31
🕐 Tue-Sun: 10am-5pm. Mon: closed.
Admission charge.

Museu Nacional do Azulejo

Rua Madre de Deus 4
☎ 01-814 77 47
🕐 Tue: 2pm-6pm. Wed-Sat: 10am-6pm. Mon, Thu, Fri and Sun: closed.
Admission charge.

Pottery on display at the Feira da Ladra

Bairro Alto and Estrela

Igreja da Santa Catarina

Calçada do Combro

The **Igreja de Santa Catarina** gives its name to its neighbourhood. The district of **Santa Catarina** is an unspoilt area in the south-west portion of the **Bairro Alto**. Its narrow winding streets and exuberant local residents give the place an authentic local character.

The church itself is a 17th-century building which was reconstructed after falling victim to the 1755 earthquake. Many of the original fixtures and fittings survived the disaster, and the baroque organ and decorative, gilded woodwork inside the church give a rare insight into what the interior architecture of Lisbon's churches was like before the earthquake.

Miradouro de Santa Catarina

Rua Marechal Saldanha

The church lies on the same hill as the **Miradouro de Santa Catarina**, a garden *belvedere* at the end of Rua Marechal Saldanha. It has spectacular views of the River Tejo and the main suspension bridge over the river, the Ponte 25 de Abril, which is named after the date in 1974 when the Salazar dictatorship was overthrown.

The garden is noted for its statue of the Adamastor. Legend has it that the Adamastor was a fearsome monster of mythic proportions which attacked Portuguese explorers, adventurers and traders as they tried to sail around the Cape of Good Hope at the southern tip of Africa on their journey to and from the Indian sub-continent.

Mercado 24 de Julho

Avenida 24 de Julho
🕐 Mon-Sat: 3am–12noon. Sun: closed.

The **Mercado 24 de Julho** is a vibrant food and flower market. Its domed central building is a landmark in the local skyline. All manner of goods arrive by engine-powered and horse-driven transport, as well as by ferry, in the early hours of the morning. The market is at its busiest at this time.

The **Jardim Botânico** occupies 4 hectares (10 acres) of sloping grounds owned by the Faculty of Science at the city's university. The gardens were established as a research resource for the department in 1873.

Many thousands of plant species are

Palácio da Assembleia Nacional

represented here, and the gardens are known especially for their flowers, cacti and trees. They are landscaped into Biblical themes, such as a glorious avenue of palm trees depicting Jesus's triumphant entry into Jerusalem on Palm Sunday. The gardens are an ideal place to enjoy a picnic on a sunny day.

The building which contains the Portuguese parliament is known as the **Palácio da Assembleia Nacional**. Its other name, Palácio de São Bento, derives from its original use at the end of the 16th century as a Benedictine monastery dedicated to São Bento. With the dissolution of religious orders in 1834 the palace took on its new function.

The building is a huge neo-classical construction with an imposing facade and an interior crammed with statues and marble pillars. A vast public park has been established at the rear of the palace which contains various state buildings, including the official residence of the Prime Minister of Portugal.

In the 1770s, the devout Maria I promised God she would commission a church if she gave birth to a son and heir. The arrival of her eldest son, José, prompted the building of the **Basílica de Estrêla** in 1779. The church was completed in 1790, but José had died from smallpox two years earlier. This caused Maria I to

Jardim Botânico

Rua da Escola Politécnica 56
☎ 01-396 15 21
🕐 Apr-Sep: Mon-Fri: 9am-6pm. Sat-Sun: 10am-6pm. Oct-Mar: Mon-Fri: 9am-8pm. Sat-Sun: 10am-8pm. Admission charge.

Palácio da Assembleia Nacional

Rua de São Bento
☎ 01-396 01 41
🕐 Visit by appointment only.

Lisbon Rooftops

Basílica de Estrêla

Largo da Estrêla
☎ 01-396 09 15
⏰ Mon-Sun: 7.30am-
1pm and 3pm-8pm.

Jardim da Estrêla

Praça de Estrêla

suffer mental illness until she died in exile in Brazil in 1816. Her body is buried in the basilica within an ornate baroque tomb.

Architecturally, the church, which is noted for its huge dome, is a simpler version of the monastery at Mafra. The view of Lisbon from the top of the dome (reached by climbing 230 steps) is well worth the effort.

The facade is made up of bell-towers and statues. Inside, the coloured marble surfaces are lit with sunlight through the pierced dome. A private side room contains a life-sized cork- and terracotta-figure Nativity scene by Machado de Castro which is worth asking to see.

The **Jardim da Estrêla**, also known as the 'Jardim Guerra Junqueiro', belongs to the basílica (see above) which is opposite the garden. It is a restful escape from the hurly-burly of the city, popular with local people for bringing their children, for having a picnic and for relaxing on any of the numerous park benches.

The garden is home to many species of birds, trees and tropical plants. An artificial lake has a statue of a small girl at its centre, and families bring toddlers to feed the fish, geese and peacocks. Visitors can enjoy a brass band during the summer. *(Largo de Estrêla.)*

The **Cemitério dos Ingleses** is the Protestant cemetery of the Anglican Church of St. George, established in 1717 under the terms of a 1654 treaty. In among the cypress trees are graves of English people, the most famous being Henry Fielding (1707–54), the author of *The History of Tom Jones*. Fielding died in Lisbon during a futile attempt to convalesce abroad, when his opinion of Lisbon as 'the nastiest city in the world' was undoubtedly coloured by his failing health. His travel account *Journal of a Voyage to Lisbon* was published in 1775, many years after his death. A small Jewish area is located at the north end of the graveyard.

Cemitério dos Ingleses

Rua de São Jorge
Ring the bell loudly for entry.

The **Casa-Museu Fernando Pessoa** is the home where the famous Portuguese poet spent much of the last 15 years of his life. The house has been converted into a museum celebrating Pessoa's life and work. It contains artwork, such as the painting of the poet by Almada Negreiros, and personal effects, such and diaries and reading glasses. Temporary exhibitions display the work of artists influenced by Fernando Pessoa's modern poetry. Pessoa was a well-known Lisbon celebrity, as shown by his bronze statue in the A Brasileira café in Rua Garret.

Casa-Museu Fernando Pessoa

Rua Coelho da Rocha 16
☎ 01-396 81 90
🕐 Mon-Wed and Fri: 10am-6.30pm. Thu: 1pm-8pm. Sun: closed.

Portugal's national art collection is located at the Casa das Janelas Verdes (the house with the green windows). The **Museu Nacional de Arte Antiga** is second only in cultural importance to the Gulbenkian Museum (page 32). Originally built for the counts of Alvor, the palace was purchased by the Marquês de Pombal and took on its new function in 1884.

D. Sebastiao, Museu Nacional de Arte Antiga

An annexe was added in 1940 on the site of the St. Albert Carmelite Monastery, ruined in the 1755 earthquake. Its only surviving element is the 16th-century chapel of St. Albert, which now forms an integral part of the museum. The collection includes excellent galleries of European art from the 14th to 19th centuries, largely donated by private collectors. Masterpieces in this section include *The Temptations of St Anthony* by Hieronymus Bosch, *The Virgin and Child and Saints* by Hans Holbein the Elder, and the Italian Renaissance painters Piero della Francesca and Raphael.

Other galleries contain Baroque to Neo-Classical furniture, textiles and other interior decoration, jewellery made from precious metals, and artefacts from Africa and the Far East. The foreign exhibits highlight how Portuguese art evolved over the centuries through the influence of its colonies. For example, the displays of Chinese and Portuguese porcelain show how ceramics have been influenced.

The top floor of the museum contains religious sculpture and Portuguese paintings. The most important of these are the 15th-century *Ecce Homo* by an anonymous Portuguese painter and the multi-panelled *Adoration of St Vincent* accredited to Nuno Gonçalves. The latter is an important symbol of national pride in the Age of Discovery.

Museu Nacional de Arte Antiga

Rua das Janelas Verdes
☎ 01-396 41 51
🕐 Wed-Sun: 10am-6pm.
Tue: 2pm-6pm
Mon: closed.
Admission charge.

Parque Eduardo VII

North Lisbon

Lisbon was the host of the **Expo 98** fair, celebrating the 500th anniversary of Vasco de Gama's first voyage to India. The theme of this ambitious event was the ocean, with the emphasis on preserving our heritage for future generations. The **Oceanário de Lisboa** was one part of the exhibition which is now a permanent aquarium, the second largest in the world.

The aquarium explores the links between sea and land in each of its five open tanks. The largest is the same size as four Olympic swimming pools and contains animals and plants from the ocean. Four smaller tanks recreate the habitat within the Antarctic, Atlantic, Pacific and Indian oceans. The aquarium contains about 25,000 animals in total.

The **Museu da Água** is housed in the city's first steam-powered pumping station, which was established in 1880. The four original engines have been preserved with one remaining in working order, albeit electrically powered.

The museum, which won a European award of excellence in 1990, charts the evolution of water-supply technology in Lisbon, particularly the city's aqueduct and fountains, through extensive documentary and photographic evidence. For example, the Chafariz d'El Rei (an early fountain in Lisbon) had six founts where people queued to get fresh water according to their social status.

The museum also commemorates the achievements of the 18th-century engineer who built the aqueduct, Manuel da Maia.

The **Parque Eduardo VII** is the largest park in Lisbon. It was dedicated to the British king Edward VII after his visit to the city in 1903 to extend the Anglo-Portuguese alliance, first negotiated in 1386. Two pillars were added to the park to commemorate a visit in 1957 by Elizabeth II.

The park itself has an area of 25 hectares (62 acres). It is a wide, grassy incline containing box hedges and several

Oceanário de Lisboa

Doca das Olivais
☎ 01-891 70 02
🕐 Mon-Sun: 10am-8pm.
Admission charge.

Museu da Água

Rua do Álviela 12
☎ 01-813 55 22
🕐 Tue-Sat: 10am-
12.30pm and 2pm-5pm.
Sun-Mon: closed.
Free admission.

Parque Eduardo VII

Praça Marquês de
Pombal
🕐 Mar-Sep: Mon-Sun:
9am-6pm. Oct-Feb:
Mon-Sun: 9am-5pm.
Admission charge.

A fountain created for Expo 98

Estufas

Praça Marquês de
Pombal
☎ 01-385 04 08
🕐 Mar-Sep: Mon-Sun:
9am-6pm. Oct-Feb:
Mon-Sun: 9am-5pm.
Admission charge.

patterned boulevards, leading to a garden at its apex. It contains a sports stadium, a lake and a children's play area.

The **Estufas** are two jungle-like, glass greenhouses in the north-west corner of the Parque Eduardo VII. The **Estufa Quente** (hot house) houses cacti, water-lilies and flamingos within its humid enclosure. The **Estufa Fria** (cold house) is landscaped with fountains, streams and ponds among the hardy blooms and ferns.

The roundabout at the top end of the Avenida da Liberdade is known as the **Praça Marquês de Pombal**. The square has a statue of the famous leader on a column at its centre, erected in 1934. Pombal has his hand on a lion, a symbol of power, and sets his eyes towards Baixa, the setting of his greatest political achievements.

The **Museu Calouste Gulbenkian** opened to the public in 1969 as a direct response to the bequest of Calouste Gulbenkian in his will to the Portuguese nation.

The multi-millionaire Armenian oil magnate settled in Lisbon after World War II and set up his foundation just before his death in 1955. The Gulbenkian Foundation is now worth over $1 billion and is without doubt the most important private source of income for Portuguese arts and culture.

Gulbenkian was a discerning collector of fine art throughout his life, but his collection gathered pace when he earned the nickname 'Mr Five Per Cent' having negotiated the sale of the Iraqi Oil

Company in the 1920s. He chose works with the help of expert advisers, chiefly for him to enjoy at home.

The museum reflects his personal tastes and falls into two broad categories: European art from the 14th century onwards and art from the East – near, middle and Orient. The European art includes early Dutch and Flemish masterpieces (such as paintings by Rogier van der Weyden), illustrated manuscripts, ivory carvings and books.

Later exhibits include 18th-century French furniture and silverware, paintings by Manet, Renoir, Turner and Rembrandt, and a room devoted to Guardi's views of Venice.

The collection of Lalique *art nouveau* jewellery is magnificent. These pieces were particularly close to Gulbenkian's heart, as he was a good firend of René Lalique himself.

The rest of the museum contains work ranging from the third millennium BC to the mid-20th century. Artefacts include pieces from ancient Egyptian, Roman, Mesopatamian and Greek civilisations. There is also a terrific collection of textiles and ceramics from Eastern cultures.

Established in 1983 within the Gulbenkian Foundation complex, the **Centro de Arte Moderna** celebrates 20th century Portuguese art. The original

for less **Museu Calouste Gulbenkian**

Avenida de Berna 45-A
☎ 01-793 51 31
🕐 Tue-Sun: 10am-5pm
Mon: closed.
Admission charge.
2 admissions for the price of 1 with voucher on page 69.

Praça Marquês de Pomba

Centro de Arte Moderna

Rua Dr Nicolau de Bettencourt
☎ 01-795 02 36
⏰ Tue, Thu, Fri and Sun: 10am-5pm. Wed and Sat: 10am-7.30pm. Mon: closed.
Admission charge.
2 admissions for the price of 1 with voucher on page 69.

Aqueduto das Águas Livres

Calçada da Quintinha
☎ 01-813 55 22
Guided tours by appointment only.

collection was a private bequest of art dating from 1910, and important works by contemporary artists have been added since.

Its most famous work is *Fernando Pessoa in the Café Irmãos Unidos* painted in 1964 by José de Almada Negreiros. International art is also represented, in particular the work of those artists influenced by their Portuguese counterparts. The centre also owns an important British collection.

The **Centro Artístico Infantil** is part of the Gulbenkian Foundation complex which houses the museum and the modern art gallery. The centre looks after children while their parents can enjoy the other attractions within the complex. It also educates and entertains the children while they are at the centre. The facility is well-stocked with games and toys, offers child care for the 4–12 age range and hosts art workshops for the very young on Saturday and Sunday afternoons. (*Rua Marquês de Sá da Bandeira, ☎ 01-7950236 ⏰ Mon-Fri: 9.30am-5pm.*)

Lisbon had no regular fresh water supply until the **Aqueduto das Águas Livres** became operational in 1748. The project also fulfilled João V's personal agenda of constructing large public structures for posterity. The aqueduct was designed to withstand an earthquake and this foresight was tested within seven years of its existence. Its creators (architect, Custódio Vieira and engineer, Manuel da

Aqueduto das Águas Livres

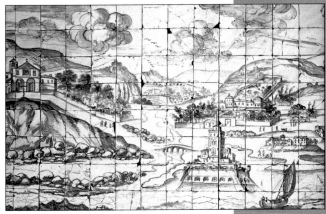

An azulejo map of old Lisbon

Maia) were subsequently commissioned by the Marquês de Pombal with many rebuilding projects in the city.

Finally completed in the 19th century, the aqueduct's total length, including secondary channels, is (56 kilometres) 36 miles. Its public walkways were closed to the public in 1853 after a series of infamous murders.

The **Palácio dos Marquêses de Fronteira** remains the private residence of the 12th Marquis, despite the fact that aristocratic titles were abolished in 1910 with the establishment of the Portuguese republic. The pink palace is known especially for the beauty of its gardens and for the excellence of it *azulejo* (tile) decorations. It was built in 1640 in a rural location to celebrate the inauguration of the Fronteira title, bestowed by Pedro II on João de Mascarenhas for his loyal service during the War of Restoration.

The guided tour includes access to selected living rooms, the library and the 16th-century chapel, the oldest part of the palace. The interior decoration makes for an interesting comparison of 17th-century *azulejo* (tile) design.

The gardens also contain beautiful tile panels, integrated with the box hedges and plants typical of Portuguese landscape gardening. The hedges are shaped to represent the seasons of the year.

Palácio dos Marquêses de Fronteira

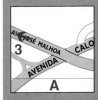

Largo São Domingos de Benfica 1
☎ 01-778 20 23
🕑 Jun-Sept: Mon-Sat: 11am-1pm. Oct-May: Mon-Sat: 10.30am-1pm. Admission charge.

Museu da Música

Rua João de Freitas Branco
☎ 01-778 80 74
🕑 Tue-Sat: 1.30pm-8pm. Sun-Mon: closed. Admission charge.

**Museu da Ciência /
Museu de História
Natural**

Jardim Botânico
R.da Escola Politécnica 56
☎ 01-392 18 00
Free admission.

**Palácio Pimenta
(Museu da Cidade)**

Campo Grande 245
☎ 01-759 16 17
🕒 Tue-Sun: 10am-1pm
and 2pm-6pm. Mon:
closed.
Admission charge.

**Museu Rafael Bordalo
Pinheiro**

Campo Grande 382
☎ 01-759 08 16
🕒 Tue-Sun: 10am-1pm
and 2pm-6pm. Mon:
closed.
Admission charge.

The new **Museu da Música** has a
collection of almost 800 musical
instruments, the earliest dating from the
16th century. The exquisite baroque
harpsichord is especially worth seeing, and
there are good examples of early string
and wind instruments. The museum
charts the development of instruments up
to the present day, with examples of 20th-
century designs. There is also a collection
of specialist literature.

The two Faculty of Science museums of
Lisbon University are housed in 19th-
century buildings in the north-western
corner of the Jardim Botânico. The **Museu
de História Natural** shows the evolution of
flora and fauna in the Iberian peninsula
since prehistoric times, and the **Museu da
Ciência** displays geological and zoological
exhibits to explain simple scientific
principles. Its interactive sections are
popular with children of all ages. Both
museums are owned by the university but
are permanently open to the public.

Lisbon University itself has had a
turbulent life. Established in 1290 by
King Dinis, it gradually became a centre of
political unrest and a force for change,
especially with regard to the monarchy.
The university engaged in a power struggle
with Manuel, who tried to impose legal
and economic sanctions on the
establishment. When these measures
failed to stop the unrest, João III
disbanded the university in 1537 and set
up a new college in Coimbra.

By the end of the 16th century, education
in the capital had passed into the hands
of the Jesuits. Lisbon had no university
within its boundaries until after the 1910
revolution, though the exiled university
had already set up the gardens in which
the museums are now housed.

The 18th-century palace, **Palácio Pimenta**,
was allegedly built by João V for his
mistress, the nun Madre Paula. It was
originally a rural mansion, but the city
limits of Lisbon have now engulfed the
palace.

The building was first used to house the
Museu da Cidade in the 1970s. The city

museum's main function is to chronicle the history of Lisbon from prehistoric times. It is especially strong on the period between the restoration of political independence (1640) and the establishment of the Portuguese Republic (1910).

The collection displays all manner of evidence in its quest to tell the story of the city: sculpture, paintings, pottery, written documents, maps, prints, models and photographs. The

Street scene with trams

artefacts depicting Lisbon as it was before the earthquake are fascinating, and include a painting by Dirk Stoop of the Terreiro do Paço (now the Praça do Comércio, page 10) and a 1950s model reconstruction of the city before 1755. Another room is dedicated to the Águas Livres aqueduct.

The **Museu Rafael Bordalo Pinheiro** stands opposite the Museu da Cidade, separated by the busy Campo Grande thoroughfare. This museum celebrates the life and work of the 19th-century artist, potter and ceramic satirist, Rafael Bordalo Pinheiro, who lived in this building.

The ground floor of the mansion contains a collection of sketches, cartoons, paintings and illustrations by the eccentric artist. The first floor includes an interesting collection of elaborately crafted dishes which feature ceramic animals such as crabs, snakes and frogs attached to the bowls and seemingly trying to escape.

The estate of the Palmela family was handed to the Portuguese state in 1975.

Museu Nacional do Teatro

Palácio do Monteiro-Mor, Estrada do Lumiar 10-12
☎ 01-756 74 10
🕐 Wed-Sun: 10am-6pm.
Tue: 2pm-6pm
Mon: closed.
Admission charge
(includes entry to Museu Nacional do Traje).

This consisted of the **Parque do Monteiro-Mor** and its 18th-century **palace**. The site is located outside the city centre, so it is not usually packed with tourists. The park is made up of gardens dominated by woodland and, close to the buildings, landscaped areas of box hedges, ponds and tropical shrubs and trees.

The palace was converted into two museums, one of which is the **Museu Nacional do Teatro** (the other is the Museu Nacional do Traje, see below) This museum hosts temporary exhibitions alongside a permanent collection of artefacts celebrating 20th-century Portuguese performing arts.

Museu Nacional do Traje

Palácio do Monteiro-Mor,
Largo Júlio Castilho
☎ 01-759 03 18
🕓 Tue-Sun: 10am-6pm
Mon: closed.
Admission charge.
(includes entry to Museu
Nacional do Teatro).

The museum displays photographs, cartoons and posters of famous actors alongside props and costumes from well-known productions. There is a section devoted to Amália Rodrigues, a famous singer in the *fado* tradition – a melancholic Portuguese style analogous to French *chansons* and American blues.

The other museum in the Palácio do Monteiro-Mor is the **Museu Nacional do Traje**. It displays a range of costumes from the Middles Ages to modern times. Many are not in a perfect state of preservation, but the museum does give a flavour of the country's history through its sense of fashion. The collection includes costumes and uniforms of soldiers, politicians, courtiers, artists, musicians and literary figures.

The museum hosts temporary exhibitions according to subject themes ranging from aristocratic to everyday dress.

An Assembly guard

Belém

Torre de Belém

The **Torre de Belém** is perhaps the most famous monument in Portugal. Commissioned by Manuel I and built between 1515–21 by the architect Francisco de Arruda, the tower is one of the least altered structures of its age in the country, and symbolises Portugal's noble past as a world power.

The tower was built as a fortress to protect the monastery (page 43) and port at Belém. It was originally located in the middle of the River Tejo, but the river changed its course and, for a period, the tower was stranded on dry land. In recent times, the river has moved again and the tower is now close to the river bank.

It is famous for being the point of departure for the Age of Discovery voyages. Explorers saw the monument as an idealised symbol of home. The statue of Virgin and Child symbolises 'Our Lady of the Safe Homecoming' and so claims protection for Portuguese sailors.

The exterior décor of the tower is striking. Seafaring symbols have been carved in stone, and Manuel I's coat-of-arms takes pride of place. The battlements bear the shields of the Order of The Knights Templar, and the Renaissance-style loggia is adorned with exquisite carvings. The interior of the tower is much plainer. The basement was used as a dungeon for political prisoners until 1828. The

Torre de Belém

Avenida da India
☎ 01-362 00 34
🕑 Tue-Sun: 10am-5pm
Mon: closed.
Admission charge.

whispering gallery on the third floor and the open roof afford panoramic views.

An early 20th-century electricity generating station is the site of the **Museu da Electricidade**. This museum showcases the industrial machinery used to generate electricity, including high-pressure and low-pressure generators and steam turbines. *(Avenida Brasilia, ☎ 01-391 81 03. ⏱ Tue-Fri: 10am-5.30pm. Sat-Sun: 10am-7.30pm. Mon: closed. Admission charge.)*

Museu de Arte Popular

Avenida de Brasilia
☎ 01-301 12 82
⏱ Tue-Sun:10am-5pm
Mon: closed.
Admission charge.

Opened in 1948, the **Museu de Arte Popular** occupies a modernist, shed-like building on the Belém waterfront, between the Padrão dos Descobrimentos and the Torre de Belém (page 39). This museum celebrates the vibrant diversity of regional folk arts and crafts in Portugal. The artefacts are displayed according to region, which is of particular interest to people planning to visit other parts of the country.

The range of exhibits is vast: the museum contains clothes, jewellery, work implements, horses' saddles, ceramics and musical instruments. Highlights include toby jugs from Aveiro, bagpipes from Mirando do Douro, baskets from Trás-os-Montes, decorative ceramic cockerels and multicoloured ox yokes from Minho, fishing tackle from the Algarve, and cow bells from Alentejo.

The museum proves the richness of Portuguese regional culture and history, together with a range of European, African, South American and Asian influences.

Padrão dos Descobrimentos

Avenida de Brasilia
☎ 01-301 62 28
⏱ Tue-Sun: 9.30am-6pm. Mon: closed.
Admission charge.

The **Padrão dos Descobrimentos** is another monument facing the River Tejo at the Belém waterfront. It was built in 1960 by the Salazar government as a monument to commemorate the Age of Discovery on the 500th anniversary of the death of Henry the Navigator.

The concrete and limestone structure stands 52 metres (170 feet) high and takes the shape of a caravel's prow. The sides of the 'ship' are adorned with statues of the people who made the Age of Discovery possible as well as the Portuguese coat of arms. At the front of the tableau is Henry the Navigator himself. Other statues of historical figures include Manuel I, the national poet Camões (clutching a copy of his epic tale, *Os Lusíadas*), the painter Nuno Gonçalves (carrying a paint palette), Afonso V (the first royal patron of the explorers), Vasco da Gama, Fernão de Magalhães (Magellan) and Pedro Álvares Cabral (all explorers).

A huge compass and map marks the voyagers' routes on the pavement on the monument's north side. Inside the structure a lift takes visitors to the sixth floor for a beautiful view of the city, and the basement holds temporary exhibitions.

The controversial **Centro Cultural de Belém** was built in 1990 as the headquarters for the 6 month long Portuguese presidency of the European Union. In 1993, the stark building became a major arts venue, specialising in concerts, theatrical

Centro Cultural de Belém

Praça do Império
☎ 01-361 24 00
🕘 Mon-Sun: 9am-9.45pm.
Admission charge.

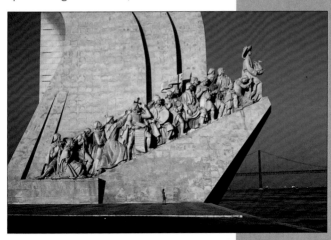

Padrão dos Descobrimentos

performances, arts lectures and temporary exhibitions, often of photography.

The **Planetário Calouste Gulbenkian** is a modern domed building next to the monastery (page 43), built in 1965 and now owned by the Portuguese Navy. The planetarium shows recreate the night sky to explain the science of outer space, with particular emphasis on star constellations and the solar system surrounding our own sun.

One specialist theme concerns the Star of

Museu de Marinha

Bethlehem (Belém in Portuguese), after which this area of Lisbon is named. English and French translations of the shows' Portuguese narratives can be followed by hiring sets of headphones.

Since 1962, the **Museu de Marinha** has been housed in the west wing of the Mosteiro dos Jerónimos (page 43). This site is providential for the maritime museum as it stands on the ground where Manuel I built a chapel to bless the explorations of which Henry the Navigator was the patron. Vasco de Gama set off from here on his historic voyage to India in 1497.

The museum charts the history of Portuguese sailing and exploration since the Age of Discovery. The main hall displays technical advances in ship-building from the 15th century onwards. It contains models of bark barges and caravels. The collection also consists of navigational aids such as early maps, astrolabes and sextants.

Other rooms show modern ships, exhibits from Portuguese colonies, and the royal living quarters on the *Amélia* (built in 1900). A separate building contains some luxurious royal barges and the sea plane, *Santa Cruz*, which flew over the South Atlantic in 1922.

The **Museu Nacional de Arqueologia** is also housed in the west wing of the monastery, along with the Museu da Marinha. This museum, founded in 1893, is the main collection and research centre for archaeology in Portugal. Exhibits are displayed from sites all over the country.

The collection includes ancient jewellery,

Planetário Calouste Gulbenkian

for less

Praça do Império
☎ 01-362 00 02
⊕ Shows: Wed, Thu: 11am, 2.30pm and 4pm (school hoildays only). Sat-Sun: 11am (for children), 3.30pm, 5pm. Admission charge.
2 admissions for the price of 1 with voucher on page 69.

ornaments and artwork from various civilisations, such as Egyptian, Roman, Etruscan, Moorish and Visigoth. The ethnological part of the museum deals with popular culture and religious themes. *(Praça do Império, ☎ 01-362 0000, ⊕ Wed-Sun: 10am-6pm. Tue: 2-6pm. Admission charge.)*

The **Museu Nacional dos Coches** occupies the east wing of the Palácio de Belém (page 44), which formerly housed the riding school of Lusitanian horses, commissioned in 1726. Queen Amélia converted the school into a national museum for royal, ecclesiastical and aristocratic coaches in 1905.

While the subject of the museum is narrow, its contents are perhaps the best of their type in Europe. Three centuries of coach design and technology can be compared directly. The main gallery displays the heaviest coaches and a smaller gallery houses two-wheeled cabs, chariots and pony traps. An upper room displays costumes, saddles and paintings of the royal family.

Manuel I promised God he would build a great monastery in celebration if Vasco de Gama succeeded in his quest to discover India. Work began on the **Mosteiro dos Jerónimos** on the explorer's return in 1502. The monastery was financed in part by a 5 per cent tax on pepper from the spice trade.

Several builders worked on the project, the most famous being Diogo de Boitac (the instigator of the Manueline style of late Gothic architecture) and his successor, João de Castilho. The monastery was given to the monks of St. Jerome before religious orders were disbanded in 1834, with a mission to offer spiritual succour

Museu de Marinha

Praça do Império
☎ 01-362 00 19
⊕ Jun-Sep: Tue-Sun: 10am-6pm. Oct-May: 10am-5pm.
Admission charge.
2 admissions for the price of 1 with voucher on page 71.

Museu Nacional dos Coches

Praça Afonso de Albuquerque
☎ 01-361 08 50
⊕ Tue-Sun: 10am-6pm
Mon: closed.
Admission charge.

Museu Nacional dos Coches

Mosteiro dos Jerónimos

Mosteiro dos Jerónimos

Praça do Império
☎ 01-362 00 34
🕓 Tue-Sun: 10am-5pm
Mon: closed.
Admission charge.

Palácio de Belém

Praça Afonso de
Albuquerque
☎ 01-363 71 41
🕓 3rd Sun of month:
morning only.
Admission charge.

to sailors and to pray for the souls of Portuguese monarchs.

The monastery is a unique example of Manueline architecture. The cloister, nave of the church of Santa Maria and the refectory are all exquisite. The cloister has decorative ballustrades and arches alongside carved images and statues. The nave's octagonal pillars and spectacular fan vaulting resembles an avenue of tall palm trees. The refectory is well-known for its 18th-century *azulejo* panels depicting the Biblical stories of Joseph and the feeding of the five thousand.

The monastery is also the pantheon for the Aviz dynasty, beginning with Manuel I and his second wife, Maria. Vasco de Gama and Luis de Camões are also buried in the chancel.

João V bought the pink marble **Palácio de Belém** in the early 18th century as a summer palace away from the centre of Lisbon. João V commissioned a new riding school and an extravagant reconstruction of the palace's interior.

The palace was slightly damaged in the 1755 earthquake (the facade collapsed) but José I and his family were unhurt. The royals then camped out in the grounds of the palace while the buildings themselves were used as a temporary hospital. The building is now used as the official residence of the President of Portugal.

The royal family's reaction to the 1755 earthquake was to move to a new palace outside the city boundaries. The palace that was eventually built for them, the **Palácio Nacional da Ajuda,** was quickly abandoned in 1807 when the family fled to Brazil under the threat of Napoleon's invasion, and it only became a permanent home to the Portuguese monarchy in 1861 when Luis I married his queen, Maria Pia.

Queen Maria Pia continued to live in the never-completed palace until 1905, after which the building became a museum containing a permanent exhibition dedicated to the Portuguese monarchy.

The fixtures and fittings are the epitome of 19th-century luxury. Examples include furniture decorated with Meissen porcelain, silk wallpaper, crystal glass chandeliers and frescoes on the ceilings. The sumptuous banqueting hall is still used for state occasions. At the other end of the palace, Luis I's neo-gothic painting studio provides an interesting insight into everyday life in the royal household.

A little west of Belém is the **Aquario Vasco da Gama**. This aquarium, which opened in 1898, exhibits a variety of species of indigenous and tropical marine life. Particular favourites, especially with children, are the turtles and seals. The adjoining museum features preserved specimens and presentations about ocean life.

Palácio Nacional da Ajuda

Largo da Ajuda
☎ 01-363 70 95
🕐 Thu-Tue: 10am-5pm
Wed: closed.
Admission charge.

Aquario Vasco da Gama

Rua Direita, 1495 Dafundo
☎ 01-419 63 37
🕐 Mon-Sun: 10am-6pm.
Admission charge.
2 admissions for the price of 1 with voucher on page 69.

Aquario Vasco da Gama

Beyond the City

The lovely town of **Sintra** lies 28 kilometres (17.5 miles) north-west of Lisbon, and should be the first port-of-call for day-trippers from the city. It was famously described by Lord Byron as a 'glorious Eden'.

The town has two parts: **Sintra Vila** and **Estefânia**. The former is famous for its museums and palace; the latter has a well-known Sunday market. Sintra gained UNESCO World Heritage site status in 1995.

The **Palácio Nacional de Sintra** (also called the Palácio Real) was commissioned by João I in 1385, on the site of an 8th-century Moorish castle. Its most obvious features are the two enormous chimneys, which were needed for the spit-roast banquets of the time. Manuel I used some of his Age of Discovery wealth to make sumptuous additions in the early 16th century.

Reflections

'...It contains beauties of every description, natural and artificial. Palaces and gardens rising in the midst of rocks, cataracts and precipices; convents on stupendous heights, a distant view of the sea and the Tagus.' - Lord Byron on Sintra, 1809

The palace remained the favourite summer retreat for the Portuguese monarchy for over 600 years. Its last official resident was Maria Pia, the grandmother of the last Portuguese king (Manuel II), who lived here until the 1880s. In 1910 the republican state turned the palace into a museum.

The palace today is an amalgam of different architectural styles. Many of the rooms are magnificent and have interesting histories. The **Sala dos Brasões** has a domed ceiling containing the crests of 74 noble families from Manuel I's reign. One crest was erased by José I after the family was executed after plotting a coup against the king.

The **Sala das Pegas** has a famous painted ceiling of 27 'chattering magpies'. João I commissioned this as a rebuke to the 27 ladies-in-waiting at court, whom he considered idle gossips and chatterers. One of the bedrooms became a prison for the mad king Afonso VI. (*Largo Rainha Dona Amélia,* ☎ *01-923 1677.* ⏰ *Thu-Tue: 10am-1pm and 2pm-5pm. Wed: closed. Admission charge.*)

Palácio Nacional de Sintra

The **Palácio da Pena** was the personal project of the 'artist king', Fernando II. He commissioned Baron von Eschwege to build an extravagant palace in a romantic, Bavarian style, within a landscaped park, as a gift to his wife.

The palace stands at the highest point of the Serra mountains on the site of a 15th-century monastery which was destroyed in the 1755 earthquake. Only the cloister and the chapel of the original building have survived. The palace is painted yellow and strawberry pink, in keeping with the styles of the time, and contains all manner of oddities from around the world.

The **ballroom** contains stained-glass windows, Far Eastern crockery and carved wooden candelabra from Asia. The entrance **arch** is hewn from the mountain rock, with its studs and crenellations giving the impression of a magic castle. The **Triton arch** is protected by a sea monster sculpture, set into the neo-Manuline portal.

The overall impression can be of expensive kitsch, but important works of art and historical artefacts abound. The 16th-century altarpiece in the **chapel** by Nicolau Chanterène tells the story of

Christ's life and Manuel II's **bedroom** is a poignant reminder of his brief reign. The palace has been unaltered since the royal family fled the country in 1910. *(Estrada da Pena (2km (1 mile) south of Sintra),* ☎ *01-923 0227.* ⏱ *Jun-Sep: Tue-Sun: 10am-6pm. Oct-May: Tue-Sun: 10am-5pm. Mon: closed. Admission charge.)*

Queluz, *en route* to Sintra from Lisbon, is the location of Portugal's most beautiful example of rococo architecture.

The **Palácio de Queluz** was transformed from a 17th-century hunting lodge into a magnificent summer palace under the direction of Mateus Vicente in 1747. The Robillion Pavilion was added later by the French architect, Jean-Baptiste Robillion.

During the latter part of the 18th century Queen Maria I lived in the palace, slowly going mad as a result of the death of her son José. Visitors to the palace at that time recorded hearing terrible shrieks and wails as she suffered hallucinations.

Highlights of the sumptuous pink palace include the **Throne Room**, adorned with gilded statues, the **Sala dos Embaixadores** with its *trompe l'oeil* ceiling, and the formal gardens, which feature box hedges, fountains and an *azulejo-* lined canal. *(Largo de Palacio, Queluz,* ☎ *01-435 00 39. Wed-Mon: 10am-1pm, 2pm-5pm. Tue: closed. Admission charge.)*

Ponte 25 de Abril, Lisbon's gateway to the south

The stretch of coast surrounding Lisbon, Sintra and Queluz and continuing north is the **Estoril Coast**, the location of several popular beach resorts.

The town of **Estoril** itself is 26km (16

miles) from Lisbon and has an affluent, leisurely atmosphere. It is home to Europe's biggest casino, a major golf course and good beaches and promenades.

Cascais, 3.2km (2 miles) along the coast, is a more vibrant resort. It attracts hoards of younger holidaymakers during the summer, has many bars, a vibrant nightlife and excellent beaches.

It was once a fishing village, and the pretty old town area has retained some reminders of this, including the daily auction of the catch at the harbour's edge. The **Museu do Mar** is devoted to Cascais' past, which is documented with photographs, paintings and treasure from local shipwrecks. (*Rua Julia Pereira de Mello, ☎ 01-484 0861. ⏱ Tue-Sun: 10am-5pm. Mon: closed. Admission charge.*)

The **Museu-Biblioteca Conde Castro Guimarães** is Cascais' finest mansion, located in the **Parque Municipal da Gandarinha** beyond the old town. The late 19th-century building overlooks an atmospheric cove and contains the furniture, paintings and books which belonged to the well-to-do Count of Castro Guimarães up to his death in 1920.

The collection includes some exquisite Indo-Portuguese furniture, *azulejos* and books dating from the 17th century. (*Avenida Rei Humberto de Italia, ☎ 01-482 5407/1. ⏱ Tue-Sun: 10am-5pm. Mon: closed. Admission charge.*)

Lisbon is connected to Southern Portugal by the huge **Ponte 25 de Abril**, the longest suspension bridge in Europe. It was built in 1966, and until the 1974 revolution was known as the Salazar Bridge. Driving across the bridge provides panoramic views of the city.

The **Cristo-Rei**, a smaller replica of Rio de Janero's Christ Statue, was built in 1959 in gratitude for the country being spared in World War II. It is located on the edge of **Cacilhas**, a little port with some fabulous fish restaurants. It is also home to the ruined fort of **Almada**, from which there are stunning views over Lisbon and Sintra.

Reflections

" ...the princess of the world...before whom even the ocean bows" - poet Luís de Camoes (1524-80), on Lisbon

Dining

Café life

The regions of Portugal have distinct characteristics which are reflected in their food and drink specialities. Lisbon offers a 'mixed menu' of all that the nation has to offer gastronomically.

In addition to Portuguese regional specialities, the city also offers Brazilian, Indian, Indonesian, Chinese, Japanese and African restaurants.

A *tasca* has the local, intimate feel of a tavern and a *cervejara* is a beer hall with snacks available, often with late opening hours. A *casa de pasto* usually serves three-course meals at a budget price whereas a *restaurante* boasts a more varied menu and formal atmosphere. A *marisquiera* specialises in fish dishes and a *churrasqueira* roasts meat on a spit – a concept imported from Brazil.

Smoking is common in most restaurants. Children are always made to feel welcome (half portions are easily arranged if not already mentioned on the menu). Vegetarians may struggle to find appropriate fare other than salads, but ethnic restaurants often serve non-meat or fish meals.

People in Lisbon often skip breakfast, which is usually a bread roll and a coffee. Lunch consists of a starter, a main course (often a dish of the day) and then fruit and/or cheese. Many locals eat from 12noon to about 2pm, so restaurants can be crowded.

Dinner is often a two-course meal eaten between 7pm and 10pm. Venues that open later than this often involve *fado* entertainment (see Nightlife, pages 54-

Casa do Leão
Portuguese restaurant

Castelo de São Jorge
☎ 01-888 01 54

Ali - A Papa
African restaurant

Rua da Atalaia 95
01-347 25 56

55). Look out for tidbits served before the starter as these are often charged for by the item eaten. Service is not usually included in the bill, and a tip of about 10% for good service is expected.

The location of Lisbon means that many local specialities involve seafood from the Atlantic Ocean. Favourite recipes often use shellfish of various types. Dried, salted cod (*bacalhau*) and grilled sardines are especially popular dishes. Other local delicacies include kale soup (*caldo verde*), pork in port (*porco à alentejana*), barbecued chilli chicken (*frango à piri-piri*), an African import, chocolate mousse and cheese made from goats' or sheeps' milk.

The wines of Portugal are developing a healthy reputation since the country joined the European Union in 1986. The reds are fruity and need to be drunk when young, and the whites tend to be light and sparkling. The most famous Portuguese alcoholic drinks are port and madeira, but the local cherry brandy should also be tasted, if only once.

Some of the best places to dine out are in the **Bairro Alto** neighbourhood, but the **Baixa** and **Belém** also have more than their fair share of good restaurants. In the margins of these pages, there are some suggestions about where to eat during your stay in Lisbon.

Canto do Camões
Fado restaurant, with show

Travessa da Espera 38
☎ 01-346 54 64

Café Martinho da Arcada
Café

Praça do Comércio 3
☎ 01-886 62 13

Al fresco dining

Shopping

The nature of the shopping experience in Lisbon is beginning to change. The traditional family small-holdings and bustling markets have been joined by modern shopping centre complexes and out-of-town hypermarkets.

This process has meant that it is becoming easier to pay for goods by credit card in Lisbon, although the traditional shops in the centre of the city still deal exclusively in cash.

Visitors resident outside the European Union are exempt from paying VAT on goods if their stay is less than 180 days. In order to claim rebates, goods should be bought at 'tax free' shops. On the presentation of a passport, sales staff give the shopper a form to fill in and give to a customs officer on leaving the country.

Lisbon is a great place to browse. The flea markets sell all kinds of food, clothes and bric à brac at affordable prices. At the other end of the spectrum, the chic Chiado and Bairro Alto quarters offer the visitor designer brands and high-quality luxury.

The Baixa neighbourhood also offers a rewarding shopping experience against a backdrop of traditional housing and cobbled streets.

Amoreiras
Shopping Centre

Avenida Engenheiro
Duarte Pacheco,
Amoreiras
☎ 01-381 02 00

O Celeiro
Food

Rua 1º Dezembro 67-83
☎ 01-342 74 95

Browsing at a flea market

Lisbon's local specialities include lace, wines, ceramics (porcelain and *azulejo*) and tapestries, all of which make excellent gifts and souvenirs.

The traditional opening hours of shops in Lisbon are from 9am to 7pm, Monday to Friday (with a two-hour lunch break from 1pm to 3pm) and 9am to 1pm on Saturdays. Some shops now remain open over lunch and on Saturday afternoons.

Shopping centre

Centro Comercial Columbo *(Avenida Lusiade Letras,* ☎ *01-711 3636.)*

Food

Charcutaria Brasil *(Rua Alexandre Herculano 84–9, Rato,* ☎ *01-388 5644.)*

Alcoholic drinks

Napoleão *(Rua dos Fanquerios 70, Baixa,* ☎ *01-887 2042.)*

Solar do Vinho do Porto *(Rua São Pedro de Alcântara 45,* ☎ *01-347 5707.)*

Music

Valentim de Carvalho *(Praça Dom Pedro IV 59, Bairro Alto,* ☎ *01-342 5895.)*

Books

Livraria Artes e Letras (second-hand) *(Largo Trindade Coelho 3, Bairro Alto,* ☎ *01-347 1675.)*

Clothes

Rosa & Teixeira (Men's tailors) *(Avenida da Liberdade 204,* ☎ *01-311 0350.)*

Ceramics

Vista Alegre (Porcelain) *(Largo do Chiado 18, Chiado,* ☎ *01-346 1401.)*

Fabrica Cerâmica Viúva Lamego *(azulejos /* ceramics) *(Largo do Intendente 25, M Intendente,* ☎ *01-885 2408.)*

Traditional crafts

Arte Rustica (Portuguese artefacts) *(Rua Aurea 246–8, Baixa,* ☎ *01-342 1127.)*

Antiques

Antiguidades Moncada *(Rua Dom Pedro IV 34, Bairro Alto,* ☎ *01-346 8295.)*

Ana Salazar
Women's designer fashion

Avenida de Roma 16F
☎ 01-848 67 99

Casa Quintão
Textiles

Rua do Alecrim 113-15, Chiado
☎ 01-346 36 86

Ricardo Hogan
Religious artefacts

Rua São Bento 281
☎ 01-395 41 02

Nightlife

Calouste Gulbenkian's arts and culture foundation has had a significant impact on Lisbon's cultural life. It is partly responsible for a thriving and diverse fusion of modern and traditional art forms and cultures. Lisbon was voted the cultural capital of Europe in 1994, in recognition of its full calendar of varied arts and entertainment activities and events.

Agência de Bilhetes para Espectáculos [ABEP]

Praça dos Restauradores
☎ 01-347 18 24

Traditional venues have box office facilities, but some events are sold out months in advance. It is advisable to check out the availability of tickets from the **Agência de Bilhetes para Espectáculos** [ABEP], a ticket booth in Praça dos Restauradores. The ABEP takes cash payments only and the tickets are handed over at the kiosk.

Teatro Nacional Dona Maria II
Theatre

Rossio
☎ 01-342 22 10

The classical music scene in Lisbon is in rude health. The city boasts several venues of international quality which provides a sophisticated programme of concerts, opera and ballet. Calendars of events produced by each venue are available at the Lisbon tourist office.

Other forms of music are well represented. The **Gulbenkian Foundation** runs an annual international jazz festival and there are several large stadiums to house big rock events. Both these musical genres also thrive in small, intimate venues all over Lisbon.

Lisbon at night

Teatro Nacional Dona Maria II

The influence of Portugal's former colonies has also had a profound effect on the richness and texture of the city's musical evolution. After the overthrow of the Salazar government through popular revolution in 1974 many of Portugal's African colonies gained their independence. This led to an increase in immigration to Portugal, and Lisbon is now home to former inhabitants of Angola, Mozambique, Capo Verde and Guinea Bissau, Goa and Brazil. Local bands have absorbed all these influences to create rich, multi-ethnic styles of music.

These bands are also quick to incorporate international musical innovations and trends. For example, rap music is now an integral part of the mix of Lisbon's youth culture. At the other extreme, *música pimba* is a hybrid genre of traditional Portuguese folk melodies and arrangements given modern-day lyrics.

Perhaps the most famous of Lisbon's musical delights is *fado*, which is a form unique to Portugal with subtle variations between regions. The word *fado* is best translated as 'fate'. Fado deals with the very Portuguese concept of *saudade*: a longing for that which has been lost or indeed never attained. This sense of 'disappointment' gives *fado* music intense emotional power. Sung well, *fado* is an unmissable experience. The Lisbon variety is earthy and melancholic whereas the

Teatro Nacional de São Carlos
Opera, ballet

Rua Serpa Pinto 9
☎ 01-346 59 14

Coliseu dos Recreiros
Large rock venue

Rua das Portas de Santo Antão
☎ 01-343 16 77

fado music of Coimbra has a distinctive, lighter touch.

Fado first came to prominence in the mid 19th century in bars, cafés and restaurants, sung by men and women rhythmically accompanied by an acoustic guitar (*viola* in Portuguese) and a mandolin-like 12-stringed instrument called a *guitarra*. The music originally grew out of the sense of homesickness felt by sailors during the Age of Discovery.

Hot Clube
Jazz, folk

Praça da Alegria 39
☎ 01-346 73 69

The intense personal atmosphere of *fado* was further developed through the tragic life and death of one its early singers, Maria Severa (1810–1836). Fado takes up many social and political themes for its expression. It remains popular and venues often offer late-night meals and drinks to accompany the evening's entertainment.

Lisbon offers plenty of other bar and nightclub activity, particularly in **Bairro Alto** and the neighbouring riverside area. Bairro Alto frequently hosts street parties although the clubs are fairly subdued. The large spaces (and lack of local residents' resistance) have spawned a vigorous dance scene in **Rato**, especially in converted warehouses and riverside wharves.

Lisbon's nightclubs offer late-night drinking hours and a wide range of popular music styles.

Evening dining

Film buffs have plenty of choice is Lisbon. Foreigners are well catered for because the national tendency is to show films in their original languages with sub-titles rather than to dub actors' voices with Portuguese translations. Tickets are usually cheap, with reductions on Mondays. Venues range from modern multiplexes to cult-movie art houses, known locally as *Cinemateca Portuguesa*.

Theatres tend to perform in Portuguese, so have less appeal for tourists.

It is always a good idea to read the listings magazines to find out what cultural entertainment is on offer in the city. Information is freely available from the tourist office.

Cinema and theatre

Amoreiras (multiplex cinema at shopping centre) *(Avenida Engenheiro Duarte Pacheco, Amoreiras. ☎ 01-381 0200.)*

Cinemateca Portuguesa (art house cinema) *(Rua Barata Salgueiro 39. ☎ 01-354 6279.)*

Music

Centro Cultural de Belém (classical) *(Praça do Império. ☎ 01-361 2444.)*

Fundação Calouste Gulbenkian (classical, international jazz festival) *(Avenida de Berna 45. ☎ 01-793 5131.)*

Pé Sujo (Brazilian music) *(Largo de São Martinho 6–7. ☎ 01-886 5629.)*

Ritz Clube (African music) *(Rua da Glória 57. ☎ 01-342 5140.)*

Johnny Guitar (small rock venue) *(Calçada Marquês de Abrantes 72. ☎ 01-396 4301.)*

Fado

Parreirinha de Alfama *(Beco do Espirito Santo 1. ☎ 01-886 8209.)*

A Severa *(Rua das Gáveas 55. ☎ 01-346 4006.)*

Adega do Machado *(Rua do Norte 91. ☎ 01-342 8713.)*

Nightclubs

Portas Largas *(Rua da Atalaia 105. ☎ 01-346 4301.)*

Frágil *(Rua da Atalaia 128. ☎ 01-346 9578.)*

Kapital *(Avenida 24 de Julho 68. ☎ 01-395 5963.)*

Luso
Fado

Travessada Queimada 10
☎ 01-342 22 81

Kapital
Disco

Avenida 24 de Julho 6
☎ 01-395 59 63

Visitor Information

Elevador da Glória

CHILDREN

Lisbon has plenty of attractions for visitors of any age. Children are well catered-for in the **Centro Artístico Infantil** (page 34), and will enjoy exploring the **Museu da Marioneta** (page 19), the **Oceanário de Lisboa** and the **Museu da Arte Popular** (page 40).

Lisbon's gardens are popular with energetic kids, and the **Parque Eduardo VII** (page 31) has a play area. They can't fail to enjoy an exciting ride on one of the city's *elevadores*.

Restaurants in this child-friendly country usually welcome children and offer child-size portions or separate menus.

CUSTOMS

Import restrictions for EU residents are: **Tobacco**: 800 cigarettes or 200 cigars; **Alcohol**: 90 litres of wine plus 10 litre of spirits.

Restrictions for non-EU residents are: **Tobacco**: 200 cigarettes or 50 cigars; **Alcohol**: 2 litres of wine plus 1 litre of spirits.

Import of coffee and tea is restricted to personal use. Visitors requiring visas are supposed to be able to prove they have enough money for their stay.

ELECTRIC CURRENT

Electricity in Portugal runs on 220V with a two-prong plug.

ETIQUETTE

It is polite to address people as *senhor* or *senhora* and to greet shopkeepers when entering and leaving shops.

Although Lisbon is a coastal town, beachwear is not usually worn in the city. Cover arms and legs when visiting churches.

The Portuguese are friendly and welcoming, but not always punctual and seldom in a hurry.

HEALTH AND SAFETY

EU nationals with form E111 are entitled to treatment from the national health service, but in some cases may have to pay and reclaim the money at a later date. All travellers are advised to take out insurance with medical cover.

Staff at pharmacies can offer advice about minor ailments, and there is a **British Hospital** in Lisbon with English-speaking doctors. *(Hospital Britânico, Rua Saraiva de Carvalho 49, 1250 Lisbon, ☎ 01-395 50 67.)*

As in any big city, guard your valuables in crowded and touristy areas, and be careful after dark.

HOTELS

Below is a selection of hotels for various budgets in or near the centre of Lisbon. 𝕤 = 7000$00 for a standard double room per night.

Baixa and Alfama

Sofitel Lisboa *(Avenida da Liberdade 123-5, MAvenida, ☎ 01 342 9202.)* 𝕤 𝕤 𝕤 𝕤 𝕤

Tivoli Lisboa *(Aveddina de Liberdade 165,1250, Mavenida, ☎ 01 319 8900.)* 𝕤 𝕤 𝕤 𝕤

Albergaria Senhora do Monte *(Calçada do Monte 39, ☎ 01 886 6002.)* 𝕤 𝕤 𝕤

Residencial Roma *(Travessa da Glória 22a, 1°, ☎ 01 346 0557.)* 𝕤 𝕤

Florescente *(Rua das Portas de Santo Antao 99, ☎ 01 342 6609.)* 𝕤

Bairro Alto and Estrela

Hotel de Lapa *(Rua do Pau da Bandeira 4,*

EMERGENCIES

Dial ☎ 112 for the Police, the Fire Service and for an ambulance.

1200, ☎ 01 396 8143.) 💰 💰 💰 💰

Lisboa Plaza *(Travessa do Salitre 7, 1250, ☎ 01 346 3922.)* 💰 💰 💰

Amazónia *(Travessa de da Fábrica dos Pentes 12-20, ☎ 01 387 7006.)* 💰 💰 💰

Borges *(Rua Garrett 198, 1200, ☎ 01 346 1951.)* 💰 💰

Residencial Camões *(Travessa de Poço da Cidade 38, 1°, ☎ 01 346 7510.)* 💰

North Lisbon

Le Meridien Lisboa *(Rua Castilho 149, ☎ 01 389 0505.)* 💰 💰 💰 💰 💰

Hotel Real Parque *(Avenida de Luis Bivar, ☎ 01 357 0101.)* 💰 💰 💰 💰

Rex *(Rua Castilho 169, 1070, ☎ 01 388 2161.)* 💰 💰 💰

Residencial Avenida Alameda *(Avenida Sidónio Pais 4, ☎ 01 353 2186.)* 💰 💰

Dom João *(Rua José Estêvão 43, Manjos, ☎ 01 524 1717.)* 💰

Belém

Hotel da Torre *(Rua dos Jerónimos 8, ☎ 01 363 6262.)* 💰 💰 💰

LANGUAGE

The Portuguese don't like to be addressed in Spanish, and are always encouraging when foreigners attempt their language. Pronunciation is quite difficult, however, as Portuguese has nasal vowels (represented by a tilde (~) over the letter). The language also has masculine and feminine forms.

Yes/No	*Sim/Nao*
Hello	*Bom dia*
Goodbye	*Adeus*
Excuse me	*Desculpe*
Please	*Por favor*
Thank you	*Obrigado/a*
Do you speak English?	*Fala inglês?*
I don't understand	*Não percebo*
Where is...?	*Onde é...?*
Entrance	*Entrada*
Exit	*Saída*

LOST PROPERTY

The lost property office is at Rua dos Anjos 56a. For items lost on the metro, contact the metro station at Restauradores *(☎ 01-342 7707).*

Open	*Aberto*
Closed	*Fechado*

LOST CREDIT CARDS

American Express *(☎ 01-315 5371)*;
Mastercard *(☎ 0501 112 72)*; **Visa** *(☎ 0501 1107)*.

MAIL / POST

The convenient **post office** opposite the tourist office at Praça dos Restauradores 58 is open from 8am-10pm Monday to Friday and from 9am until 6pm at weekends. From here you can send overseas mail and use the fast express service of the national postal service (*Correios*).

Poste Restante mail, however, should be sent to the **main post office** at Praça do Comércio *(☎ 0500 6868)*, which is open from 8.30am-6.30pm Monday to Friday. Always take your passport when collecting mail, and a small charge will be made.

Correio normal refers to ordinary mail and airmail letters, which should be posted in the red post boxes. The blue boxes are for *correio azul*, or express post, which is more expensive.

Stamps are available from post offices, machines, kiosks and shops displaying the *Correios-selos* sign.

MONEY

There are 100 *centavos* to an *escudo ($)*. Amounts are written with the $ sign in the place of the decimal point, eg. 200$00 is 200 *escudos* and no *centavos*. 1000$00 is often referred to as a *conto*. Banknotes come in denominations of 10,000$00, 5,000$00,

Post boxes

2,000$00, 1,000$,00 and 500$00. There are 200$00, 100$00, 50$00, 20$00, 10$00, 5$00, 2$50 and 1$00 coins.

Travellers cheques are expensive to cash, but are the safest way to carry money. They can be cashed in banks, but additional transaction fees are higher than in *bureaux de change*. Eurocheques often work out cheaper.

Major credit cards, of which the most popular is Visa, are accepted in large shops, hotels and in the more touristy restaurants.

OPENING HOURS

Banks - Standard opening hours are 8.30am to 3pm Monday to Friday.

Restaurants - Lunch is normally served between 12noon and about 3pm. Dinner is from 7pm until 10pm or later. Even restaurants which claim to open all day may close for a few hours before dinner.

Museums / Galleries - Most museums are closed on Mondays. This guide lists individual opening times under each museum's entry.

Shops - Business hours are generally 9am-1pm and 3pm-7pm Monday to Friday, and Saturday 9am-1pm. Many of the shops in the most touristy parts of the city, including Baixa, are beginning to stay open a lunchtimes and on Sundays. Shopping centres open until about 11pm.

LOST CREDIT CARDS

American Express (☎ 01-315 5371);
Mastercard (☎ 0501 112 72); **Visa** (☎ 0501 1107).

Shopping for souvenirs

The main post office

PACKING

Summer is the popular time to visit Lisbon, and care should be taken to protect skin against the average 11 hours a day of sunshine that the city receives in June, July and August. Temperatures in the height of summer can reach over 30°C (85°F) and the city is very humid. The winter months are the rainiest, but temperatures are mild.

Visitors taking excursions to nearby Sintra (page 46) should be aware that the area is considerably damper and cooler throughout the year.

SPECIAL TRAVELLERS

Disabled - Facilities are slowly improving for disabled visitors. The transport agency Carris runs a minibus service from 7am to 12midnight, but this usually has to be booked at least 2 days ahead and is really not much cheaper than a taxi. *(☎ 01-758 5676.)*

The **Secretariado Nacional de Rehabilitaçao** *(Avenida Conde de Valbom 63, ☎ 793 6517)* publishes the *Guia de Turismo para Pessoas com Deficiências* (Tourist Guide for Disabled People) which gives advice and lists helpful numbers. It is available from the address above.

Elderly - Where specified in this guide, *for*

LUGGAGE STORAGE

You can put baggage into storage at the **airport** between 5am-2am, and at **Rossio** *(Praça dos Restauradores, ☎ 01-343 3747)* **Cais do Sodré** *(☎ 01-347 0181)* and **Santa Apolónia** *(☎ 01-848 4025)* railway stations from 6am until 2am.

TAXES

Non-EU citizens can claim VAT back on goods over 12,000$00 purchased from shops in the Europe Tax-Free Shopping Portugal scheme. Refunds are given at customs when leaving the country.

less discounts are available on top of reduced senior prices.

Students - Concessions are available at many attractions and museums when acceptable ID, such as an ISIC card, is produced. Where specified in this guide, *for less* discounts are available on top of the normal student discount.

Gay - Recent years have seen dramatic changes in the way Lisbon treats its gay and lesbian community both legally and socially. **ILGA-Portugal**, Lisbon's gay organisation, can be contacted at Apartado 21281, Lisboa Codex 1131, and has a useful website *(ilga portugal@ilga.org)*.

TELEPHONES

Public telephones accept 10$00, 20$00, 50$00, 100$00 and 200$00 coins. Some older ones take only the first three. Telephone card phones also exist, and cards can be purchased from post offices, newsagents and tobacconists in denominations of 50 and 120 units.

Calls made from hotels are often expensive, but post offices offer a service where you make your call and then pay at the counter. Cheap times for telephoning are evenings and weekends.

TIPPING

Tips of around 10% are expected by waiting staff and taxi drivers. Toilet/restroom attendants should be given 25-50$00, and porters 100$00 per item carried.

ICEP

Palázio Foz in Praça dos Restauradores
☎ 01 346 6307

TOURIST INFORMATION / LISTINGS

The main *turismo* office of **ICEP** (Investimentos, Comércio e Turismo de Portugal) (ICEP) is in the Palázio Foz in Praça dos Restauradores *(☎ 01 346 6307)* and opens every day from 9am-8pm. It is a good source of information about tours, hotels, venues and events. There is also a branch of the *turismo* at the airport, open 6am-2am *(☎ 849 43 23/849 36 89)*.

The offices stock several useful free publications about what's on in the city. The *TIPS* booklet is a good general listings guide, *What's on in Lisbon and the Estoril Coast* is published monthly, and the

Queuing for a bus

comprehensive Real Lisbon guide can be purchased. Ask if you can't see any of these on display.

TOURS

Coach tours - Several companies in the city offer guided day trips or longer tours to places of interest outside the city and further afield, as well as night tours of Lisbon itself and orientation tours which include dinner. Contact the *turismo* for details.

Open-top bus tours - The **'Circuito Tejo'** takes in most of Lisbon's major sites and runs hourly from May to September between 11am to 4pm. With your ticket you can hop on and off all day. (☎ 01-363 93 43).

River trips - From April to October, Gray Line runs multilingual boat trips along the Tejo river to Belém and back without stopping. Departure is at 3pm from the Terreiro do Paço ferry terminal.

Tourist tram tour - This leaves from Praça do Comércio at least twice a day from March to October and takes passengers on an hour-and-a-half long tour of the hills of Baixa and Alfama. There is also a tour which goes to Belém. (☎ 01-363 20 21).

Walking tours - Guided tours of the city on foot start from the main *turismo* office in

TELEPHONE CODES

The country code for Portugal is ☎ 351.

The code for Lisbon is ☎ 01, which must be added when making calls from outside the city.

Cais do Sodré

TRANSPORT FROM THE AIRPORT

Portela Airport is 7km (4 miles) from the city. The Aerobus departs every 20 minutes from 7am until 9pm from outside the international terminal and stops at several of Lisbon's central squares, including Praça do Comércio, Praça dos Restauradores and the station at Cais de Sodré. The ticket is then valid for a day's travel on the city's buses and trams. The journey takes about 35 minutes.

Praça dos Restauradores and explore the areas of particular historical and cultural interest. The **Old Lisbon** walk, which covers the ancient Alfama and Castelo areas, takes place on Mondays, Wednesdays and Fridays. The **Medieval Suburbia** walk takes in Bairro Alto and Carmo and is on Tuesdays, Thursdays and Saturdays. Both walks begin at 9am and last about 3 hours, and are run by **Walking Around Lisbon** (☎ *01-340 45 39*).

TRANSPORT AROUND THE CITY

Bus - Buses are run by the municipal transport company, Carris. They run from 6pm to 1am and there is an additional night-time service. Tickets are cheaper if purchased from the Carris kiosks before boarding the bus. One- or multi-day tickets are available and can also be used on trams and funiculars.

Car - Driving is not recommended, as parking is difficult, many roads are one-way and Lisbon natives can be aggressive when behind the wheel. Portugal has more road deaths for its size of population than any other European nation.

Funicular - Lisbon's *elevadores* are run by Carris. Though quite an expensive way to travel short distances, the funiculars offer stunning views.

Metro - The *Metropolitano* is the cheapest and quickest way to travel around the city, though it is still undergoing expansion. The metro runs from 6am to 1am and the entrances to stations are clearly marked with a red M.

Tickets can be purchased at stations. It is cheaper to purchase a carnet of 10 and cheaper still to get a daily or weekly pass. Metro tickets are not interchangeable with bus and tram tickets.

Trams - Trams are run by Carris and are a quintessential Lisbon experience. Line 28 provides quite a good sightseeing tour of the Castelo, and line 15 serves Belém. The pre-World War I trams are far more charming than their modern replacements.

Taxis - Compared to many cities, taxi fares are quite cheap, but care must be taken to avoid being overcharged. Most taxis are beige, and the lights on the roof indicate rates – two green lights warn that the higher tariff for weekends and evenings will be charged.

Walking - Exploring Lisbon by foot can be very pleasant except in the middle of summer when the heat makes it uncomfortable. Bear in mind, too, that the city is built on hills and a certain level of fitness may be required.

USEFUL TELEPHONE NUMBERS

Airport Information - ☎ *(01-841 3700)*.

Bus Terminal - ☎ *(01-354 5775)*.

International Directory Enquiries - ☎ *(098)*.

Local Directory Enquiries - ☎ *(118)*.

Police (24 hours) - ☎ *(01-346 61 41)*.

Railway Information - ☎ *(01-888 40 25)*.

CREDITS

Principal photography:
A.F. Kersting, Photobank, Luis Saraiva.

Flower seller

Index

Museu-Escola de Artes Decorativas

2 admissions for the price of 1 at the **Museu-Escola de Artes Decorativas** (page 20)

Valid from March 1, 1999

Centro de Arte Moderna

2 admissions for the price of 1 at the **Centro de Arte Moderna** (page 33)

Valid from March 1, 1999

Aquário Vasco da Gama

2 admissions for the price of 1 at the **Aquário Vasco da Gama** (page 45)

Valid from March 1, 1999

Museu Calouste Gulbenkian

2 admissions for the price of 1 at the **Museu Calouste Gulbenkian** (page 32)

Valid from March 1, 1999

Planetário Calouste Gulbenkian

2 admissions for the price of 1 at the **Planetário Calouste Gulbenkian** (page 41)

Valid from March 1, 1999

O portador deste voucher tem direito ao seguinte desconto no **Museu-Escola de Artes Decorativas** (page 20):

2 por 1 entrada: uma entrata livre com a compra de uma entrada de igual ou mais alto valor

O portador deste voucher tem direito ao seguinte desconto no **Centro de Arte Moderna** (page 33):

2 por 1 entrada: uma entrata livre com a compra de uma entrada de igual ou mais alto valor

O portador deste voucher tem direito ao seguinte desconto no **Aquário Vasco da Gama** (page 45):

2 por 1 entrada: uma entrata livre com a compra de uma entrada de igual ou mais alto valor

O portador deste voucher tem direito ao seguinte desconto no **Museu Calouste Gulbenkian** (page 32):

2 por 1 entrada: uma entrata livre com a compra de uma entrada de igual ou mais alto valor

O portador deste voucher tem direito ao seguinte desconto no **Planetário Calouste Gulbenkian** (page 41):

2 por 1 entrada: uma entrata livre com a compra de uma entrada de igual ou mais alto valor

Museu de Marinha

2 admissions for the price of 1 at the **Museu de Marinha** (page 42)

Valid from March 1, 1999

Customer Response Card

We would like to hear your comments about the *Lisbon for less Compact Guide* so that we can improve it. Please complete the information below and mail this card. One card will be picked out at random to win a free holiday.

No stamp is required, either in Portugal or your own country.

Name: ....

Address: ....

....

....

Tel. no.: ....

If you bought the book, where did you buy it from?........

....

If you were given the book, which tour operator gave it to you?...

Number of people travelling in your party? ....

How many days were you in Lisbon? ....

Did you like the guidebook?..

....

....

What did you like about it?...

Would you recommend it to a friend?............................

Would you be more interested in a tour operators' package if you knew it included the *Lisbon for less Compact Guide*? ....

Any other comments...

....

....

....

....

O portador deste voucher tem direito ao seguinte desconto no **Museu de Marinha** (page 42):

2 por 1 entrada: uma entrata livre com a compra de uma entrada de igual ou mais alto valor

NE PAS AFFRANCHIR

NO STAMP REQUIRED

RESPONSE PAYEE
GRANDE-BRETAGNE

Metropolis International (UK) Limited
222 Kensal Road
LONDON, GREAT BRITAIN
W10 5BN

By air mail
Par avion

IBRS/CCRI NUMBER: PHQ-D/2560/W